GOD, MALE AND FEMALE?

*Healing our Image of God,
Healing our Image of Ourselves and One Another*

CATHERINE TOON, MD

GOD, MALE AND FEMALE? by Catherine Toon, MD
Published by Imprint Publishing
PO Box 63125 Colorado Springs, CO 80962-3125
United States
www.catherinetoon.com
Phone: (724) 677-6801
Email: info@catherinetoon.com
All rights reserved. This book or parts thereof may not be reproduced in any form, stored in a retrieval system, or transmitted in any form by any means electronic, mechanical, photocopy, recording, or otherwise without prior written permission of the publisher, except as provided by United States of America copyright law.
Copyright © 2023 by Catherine Toon
All rights reserved.
ISBN 978-0-9995910-9-3 (Paperback Edition)
ISBN 978-0-9998635-0-3 (Kindle Edition)
Library of Congress Control Number 2022906924
Credits and Permissions are listed below and are considered a continuation of the copywrite page.
Printed in the United States of America
First Printing March 2023
Credits and Permissions:
Scripture taken from the Holy Bible, NEW INTERNATIONAL VERSION, NIV. Copyright 1973, 1978, 1984, 2011 by Biblica, Inc. Used by permission. All rights reserved worldwide.
Scripture quotations taken from the New American Standard Bible (NASB), Copyright 1960, 1962, 1963, 1968, 1971, 1972, 1973, 1975, 1977, 1995 by The Lockman Foundation. Used by permission. www.Lockman.org
Scripture quotations taken from the Amplified Bible (AMP), Copyright 2015 by The Lockman Foundation. Used by permission. www.Lockman.org
Scripture quotations taken from the Amplified Bible (AMPC), Copyright 1954, 1958, 1962, 1964, 1965, 1987 by The Lockman Foundation. Used by permission. www.Lockman.org
Scripture quotations marked (Mirror Bible) are taken from THE MIRROR. Copyright © 2012. Used by permission of The Author
Scripture taken from the New King James Version. Copyright 1982 by Thomas Nelson. Used by permission. All rights reserved.
Scripture taken from The Voice. Copyright 2012 by Ecclesia Bible Society. Used by permission. All rights reserved.
Scripture taken from the King James Bible is Public domain and may be used freely, without restriction and without prior permission.
Scripture quotations are taken from the Holy Bible, New Living Translation, copyright 1996, 2004, 2007, 2013, 2015 by Tyndale House Foundation. Used by permission of Tyndale House Publishers, Inc., Carol Stream, Illinois 60188. All rights reserved.
Scripture quotations marked TPT are from The Passion Translation®. Copyright © 2017, 2018 by Passion & Fire Ministries, Inc. Used by permission. All rights reserved. ThePassionTranslation.com.
Scripture quotations marked (TLB) are taken from The Living Bible copyright 1971. Used by permis-

sion of Tyndale House Publishers, Inc., Carol Stream, Illinois 60188. All rights reserved.
Verses listed without translation references are partially quoted or inferred.
[Scripture quotations are] from the New Revised Standard Version Bible, copyright © 1989 the Division of Christian Education of the National Council of the Churches of Christ in the United States of America. Used by permission. All rights reserved.

Editing by Zoe Isaacs and Bethany Millar,
Front Cover Image, Book Design, & Graphic Design by Alexix Reianne Creative
Biography Photography by Sydney Ahn Photography
Photography https://silkie.org/do-chickens-nurse-their-young.html

ENDORSEMENTS

"Dr. Toon's book is simply a treasure. Simple in that it is accessible to any of us, and a treasure because it delivers a wealth of needed clarity and perspective. Her work has helped me to better understand the nature of God and what it means to be human. I am deeply grateful."

— **Paul Young, author of The Shack**

"Dr. Catherine Toon has done significant scholarly work in her book on the divine masculine and feminine. I was already on board with her conclusions before reading, yet she has added tremendous weight to this topic and brought beautiful details to light. I am excited to see this work impact the church."

— **Dr. Jonathan Welton, Best-Selling author**

"All of Catherine Toon's teachings and books carry with them God's beautiful spirit, and this book is no exception. I am amazed by Catherine's ability to take a difficult subject and make it easy to understand. *GOD, MALE AND FEMALE? Healing our Image of God, Healing our Image of Ourselves and One Another* unpacks a topic that can be seen as complicated by so many, yet Catherine makes it accessible and easy to digest. Her interpretation of scripture is well researched and miles deep, and through her writing, we gain powerful revelation about who God is and how we can apply that truth to our life so we can come into deeper agreement and alignment with Him. I believe that everyone who reads this book will have a more profound understanding of God and also be able to rest in who He has created us to be."

— **Alana Palm, Wake Up Joyful Ministries**

"Dr. Catherine Toon boldly and yet so gently hits on a subject that many in the church world are afraid to talk about in her book *God, Male and Female?*. The idea that God is both male & female in image and likeness for some reason scares people, even though Genesis 5:2 so plainly tells us this, for when God created Adam/humankind in His/Her image, God created them male/female and called THEM Adam. Catherine weaves a beautiful depiction of this in her book, showing us the wonder of the glory of God revealed in humankind by seeing God through the lens of both genders functioning in union as one. I have taught for many years that God created Adam/humankind both genders, and then God took the 'Fe' out of the Male and formed a female who now carries a fetus, and when a Male becomes one with a Female, they return to the original design of creation and then co-create with God. The Apostle Paul called this a mystery in marriage between husbands and wives and said that it is a picture of Christ and the church, and Paul refers to the church as a she. So, for those who believe that women should not have authority or teach in the church, just know that when Jesus left the planet, He left a woman/church in charge. I want to encourage leaders, as well as all who are hungry for truth, to get a copy of this book and feed on the depth revealed in it. Catherine also did an excellent job scholastically by being very thorough in the Greek and Hebrew tenses and solid exegesis. I have known Catherine for several years and believe in her and her family and endorse this book wholeheartedly."

— Rev. Jamie Englehart, author and bishop, Connect International Ministries

"Dr. Catherine Toon is a friend and fellow co-worker in helping people like you and me to know and love God. This, her newest book, is another valuable tool to that end. She simply helps us engage eternal life by knowing God better. *God, Male and Female?* is an easy-to-read but profound presentation featuring an oft-neglected facet of scripture. In wisdom, Father God chose two primary languages to capture and share written revelation with the world: Hebrew and koine Greek. Both languages are *gendered* (meaning each word carries either a masculine, feminine, or neuter designation). This choice was obviously purposeful on God's part, yet we in the non-gendered, English-speaking West are rarely encouraged to explore this significant aspect of Holy Spirit's work in inspiring Scripture.

Catherine addresses this neglect with simple, straightforward exposition of passage after passage. She focuses on those familiar and not-so-familiar passages that speak directly of God's nature and creative/redemptive actions. The result of this study is a compelling case to look freshly at God—Father, Son, and Spirit—as the very source of our own male/female identity, equality, and distinction. The *fruit* of such a fresh look at God's own male/female nature and attributes (directly from scriptures in the original gendered languages) will almost certainly affirm your personal value plus the value of others in your life—both women and men."

— Larry A. McKnight, pastor of Joyland Church, JoylandLife.com

"There is no more important or profound study for any of us to undertake than to delve into the very nature and character of God. Because what we believe about God determines what we believe about one another and about ourselves. In this insightful work, my friend Catherine Toon helps to illuminate the Divine fullness of God within every man and woman using a strong dose of scripture and ample spiritual insight. Thank you, Catherine, for this wonderful gift."

— Keith Giles, author of the "Jesus Un" book series and Sola Mysterium: Celebrating the Beautiful Uncertainty of Everything

"Another important book by Dr. Catherine Toon from the heart of God. Her closeness to God and the time she spends in prayer, study, and reflection can be felt through every word. This timely work brings deep insight into another facet of God our Father while addressing an issue that is so important in today's culture. There is so much healing needed around the issue of gender and what God intended; Dr. Catherine's work brings us one step closer to being able to freely celebrate the differences between male and female while understanding how God beautifully brings them together within His image."

— **Elizabeth Nader, author of Master Your Mindset the Master's Way**

"This amazing book is not for the faint of heart. Catherine does another amazing job (like *Marked by Love*) of taking us on a journey of understanding God with new lenses to look through. If viewed simply through theological lenses, you will miss the richness of the experience. This book is intended to be personal and relational, to take you into your heart to experience the Godhead in ways that you may have not seen before. From Genesis through the New Covenant, Catherine weaves a tapestry of God that stays true to the premise of the book and causes you to see the magnificence of a God in fresh ways that are needed at this time in the body of Christ. Sit back, open up, and grab a drink and a journal. Be ready to be challenged to change by experiencing *God, Male and Female?*"

— **Nathan Blouse, founder of The Safe Place Ministries**

"When I began reading, I was not sure what direction Catherine's book would go! I was pleasantly intrigued by how she carefully unpacked and gently exposed so many misunderstandings surrounding this delicate subject. If this topic is open for exploration in your heart and mind, then you are in for a treat as Catherine brilliantly expands your understanding in ways you 'may not have seen coming.' A 'must read' for any serious 'searcher' for a 'more hope-filled' perspective."

— **Mike Zenker, pastor, teacher, chaplain, and celebrant, serving at Still Growing in Grace Ministries + Hope Fellowship in Elmira, Ontario Canada**

*So God created humankind in his image,
in the image of God he created them;
male and female he created them.*

Genesis 1:27 (*New RevisedStandard Version*)

CONTENTS

INTRODUCTION..21

1: GOD IN GENESIS, GOD BEFORE TIME......................33

2: IN CHRIST MASCULINITY AND FEMININITY............45

3: GETTING WISDOM..55

4: THE BATTLE OF THE SEXES AND GOD.....................65

5: FEMININE EXPRESSIONS OF THE MASCULINE......81

6: SUMMING UP..103

7: YOUR TURN: ENCOUNTERING GOD,
   MASCULINE AND FEMININE......................................109

GOD ENCOUNTER BREAK................................117

INTRODUCTION

Why This Book?

Humanity is in need in unprecedented ways. Suffering because of brokenness and confusion has been a constant, ever since the fall of humankind. The ways men/boys and women/girls see themselves are the ways they will treat themselves and one another. We will never rise above our most healthy and whole way of seeing ourselves and each other. God, the Lover of our souls and utterly good Creator, is the only One with perfect vision. He knows how He crafted every person and each gender, exquisitely and powerfully, to the minutest detail. It is personal and universal. He knows what wholeness in humanity is to look like and how to help us get there from where we are. He also knows what we share within each gender and between each gender.

We have been confused and broken about who we are and how we function as fully alive men/boys and women/girls. We have harmed one another and harmed ourselves. To be healed in how we see ourselves and how we relate to one another, we must go back to our original design. We neither created nor designed ourselves. God created us in *His* image and likeness. The mystery of maleness and femaleness is represented in the mystery of the Godhead. To be healed, whole, and thriving in our humanity, we must look there.

Chucking Our Boxes

God is fascinating—majestic, limitless, knowable, but enigmatic. Everything in creation originates with God, including us. In this book, I will be exploring God and His male and female expressions. I used the term *explore* because, in all humility, I realize that it would be ludicrous and prideful to label any exploration of God as *definitive*. Particularly in western culture, we have a need to figure things out and tuck them into well-defined boxes. We have a hard time with mystery and being okay with holding the tension of understanding that seems in conflict. But God is paradoxically knowable and ungraspable, at least with our human minds.

Moreover, humanity—regardless of culture—has a propensity to get trapped in our limited perspectives. This often amounts to what Jesus referred to as the *traditions of men* (Mark 7:7–9 and Col. 2:8). Because God reveals and expresses Himself with both male and female attributes, moving forward, I will refer to God as He/Her (Him/Her and Himself/Herself). This is on purpose to shake us out of relating to God in strictly masculine terms. I recognize this is likely to rub up against or flat-out grate against some of our deepest traditional perspectives. My intent is not to buck, dishonor, rile, or divide, but instead to invite into a delightful, expansive discovery about the nature of God that is, as you will see, solidly scriptural.

I do not approach this study cavalierly. I have been studying and grappling with this for years. As I was discussing what to do with all this study, God admonished me that it is time to share, saying:

> *I want you to teach on My dual feminine and masculine nature. I AM above the gender issue, and it is important that My kids grow in seeing Me rightly. I AM neither male nor female but engender both.*

Personal Confessions

Growing up in my family of origin, like so many families, there was a tremendous amount of instability. My father had a markedly traumatic background. I remember him, in his masculine brokenness, asserting that *everything* was sexual. And he acted out of that assertion, with devastating consequences all around. The solid strength, safety, protectiveness, and affirmation of a father and husband was almost never expressed. My mother, with her own history, had learned to survive as a strong, independent woman, as did generations before her. She proudly identified herself as a feminist (second-wave—equal pay for equal work). I learned the message that, regardless of what was said, women in "feminine roles" were essentially subjugated, sexualized servants and that "male roles" were the ones of *true* value. Accordingly, when I had a choice of "Home Economics" or "World of Construction" classes in junior high, I chose the latter—not out of true interest or personal freedom, but because I had something to prove. My construction projects were particularly dismal, as I had no genuine interest. I remember my teacher Mr. Geyer would kindly smile and nod while passing me for my effort, regardless of its dubious nature. To this day, sewing or knitting the simplest thing is definitely a "hire-out". I really could have used those "Home Economics" skills. Roles fraught with agendas and sexual abuse against the backdrop of cultural sexual revolution brought overwhelming pain and confusion about the value of women vs. men.

We were too intellectual for Christianity in our household. Nevertheless, I had profound encounters with Jesus at a very early age that planted deep seeds and, in a very real sense, preserved sanity. I learned in my core the simplicity that this Man, Whose name I did not know loved me, and I loved Him. I was drawn to my Bible, despite my father's disdain for it. I would "sneak read" about God.

The problem was that, on a surface level, God was distinctly presented as *only* male, and how masculinity had been presented to me was traumatically toxic. Women, with a few exceptions, were rarely highlighted and were painted overtly or covertly in a second-class, peripheral way—defined and confined by men.

Then enter the church, which sometimes because of and often despite its best intentions addressed women in terms of headship, submission, traditional roles, male-only Pastor CEOs, gag rules for women, and the blaming of women for the fall of humanity and for the lustfulness of men, etc. Women got a nod on Mother's Day and during a "Women in the Bible" series, but the rest of the year, church was male-dominated. Dang! It was not looking good! But deep inside, there was this gorgeous, glorious God, Who was wild about me and I about Him. He was all good and all light. He had no condescending, peripheralizing air about my being female. And He never bashed men for being male. His maleness was safe and good and protective. He celebrated my femininity without limiting me in it and had the exquisite gentleness and nurturing nature of a mother. If my pain, bondage, and confusion about so many things, including issues surrounding masculinity and femininity, was ever going to be healed, this beautiful, strong, loving God was the One to do so. And masterfully, brilliantly, and *relentlessly*, He has done just that.

He healed and firmly established my heart and mind about His premium for His daughters, *as well as* His sons, long before I was able to see it reverberating over and over *and over* in scripture. There are things you know in your heart and spirit that your mind has not caught up with yet. God reveals from the inside out. First and foremost, He wants to reveal Himself in order for us to see ourselves in our masculinity and femininity rightly.

What I Am NOT Saying and Doing

At the get-go, let me tell you what I am *not* saying and doing. I am *not* abandoning scripture in order to reflect God in a human-made, agenda-driven image. That would not bring freedom, but rather even *more* confusion, bondage, and brokenness—God forbid! I actually will be pressing scripture *hard*, while simultaneously leaning into Holy Spirit as the Helper to help. I take a high view of scripture, letting it and Holy Spirit either confirm conventional understanding or challenge our deep-seated traditions that actually put God in a box.

Much of our traditional orthodoxy from church fathers and mothers has withstood millennia of questioning and frank assault. This is amazing! I am so grateful for a secure and firm foundation that transcends a crazy world where *everything* seems up for grabs! However, there are traditions that are indeed confused, broken, and unfortunately are all too often fraught with toxic and unholy agendas. Jesus Himself said in John 16:12–13:

> [12] *I have* **much more to say to you, more than you can now bear.** [13] *But when he, the* **Spirit of truth,** *comes, he will* **guide you into all the truth.** *He will not speak on his own; he will*

speak only what he hears, and he will tell you what is yet to come.

New International Version (emphasis mine)

If we agree (and certain camps in Christianity don't) that Holy Spirit still is speaking and leading us into all truth in our understanding of scripture, God, one another, our world, etc., we can agree that it is prideful to think we have it all figured out. When we fail to enter godly questioning of what we have *assumed* is truth, we inevitably end up with limitation or frank brokenness. Traditional teaching methods of rabbis, as seen with *the* Rabbi, Jesus, involve using questions to bring up heart issues (Matt. 16:5, 21:31; John 10:36).

God *loves* engagement with His/Her kids. Bringing *any* honest question to God is honoring because we are engaging and looking to Him/Her for answers. I say "honest" because, if our questions are motivated by the agenda to entrap or accuse others, or to puff up or justify ourselves, these questions are dishonorable. But questioning our traditions does *not* dishonor God. God speaks for Himself/Herself and is not limited by *any* of our traditions. Don't you love it?!

When we feel threatened by honest questions, we have to wonder why we feel *we* have to defend God (kind of silly when you think about it) or if it is really our traditions, our need to be right, or our religious system that we are defending.

Let God be true and every man/woman a liar (Rom. 3:4). When only Christ and the Father of all humanity, in the anointing of Holy Spirit, and everything that is in line (all humanity healed into Christ's image) pointing to Them remains, that is everlasting life, light, and truth. It is unshakable, eternal, and beautiful. Let the rest be shaken and fall away. This is the redemption of all things—heaven on earth (Eph. 1:7–10; Phil. 2:9–11; Rom. 3:23–24; Col. 1:13, 19–20)!

Confusion about gender identity, roles, and sexuality—so intrinsically wrapped up with how we relate to ourselves and one another—results in human bondage, whether insidious or overt. God, expressed in Christ and through Holy Spirit, is always our starting, ongoing, and ending point. He/She *is* Truth that sets us free, whether regarding gender, sexuality, or any other concern. Having debates apart from revelation about original design is pointless and foolish (Ps. 14:1, 85:8; John 15:5). We may be little "g" gods created in the image and likeness of big "G" God (Ps. 82:6, John 10:34–36, and Gen. 1:26–27), but we simply do not know better than our Father/ Elder Brother/ Bridegroom/ Friend!

Another thing that I am *not* saying/doing is watering down the maleness of God. I am in love with His (Her) masculine nature. Humanity *desperately* needs the wholeness of the holiness of Who God is in masculine expression (as well as feminine expression). There is a holy reason "Father" and not "Mother" is used (at least overtly) and that Christ came in *masculine* not *feminine* human form. I love that and want to honor what God set up in His/ Her wisdom and for the benefit of all of humanity as His/Her kids. My happy agenda is to honor God and promote healing, freedom, and growth for every child of God. That necessitates an understanding of the femininity *as well as* the masculinity of God.

I also will not make sweeping generalizations and am not focusing on the embroiled issues of human sexuality and gender identity. This is a study about God. He/She is our intoxicating focus. He/She is the One to reveal our gender and sexuality issues to us. And He/She is the One to heal us in our struggles. None of that can happen unless we know God more accurately.

In part of our study, I explore the grammatical gender (or lack thereof) of many Greek and Hebrew nouns. The value here is not to emphatically assign biological sex, but to explore the masculinity and femininity nuances in the chosen word. For example, the Greek word for truth, *alētheia*, is actually a feminine noun, whereas the Greek word for Word, is *logos*, a masculine noun. Does this mean that the female gender has the lock on truth - definitely not?! Nor does it mean that Christ as the masculine Word excludes the feminine! Christ, *as* the Word of Truth, is masculine expressed in the feminine.

It is about the poetry and multifaceted mystery of the Trinity. We miss this in our emphatic, linear western way of thinking. In particular, the English language is not very gender specific. Other languages, such as French, bring out the masculinity or femininity of the language in a more overt way. For example, *colombe* in French, meaning dove, is a feminine noun, not because all doves are feminine, but because they behave in a feminine way. When we get to exploring Greek and Hebrew words, if you will approach it as poetry, and a mystery to explore, you will be able to celebrate the beauty and wonder of God and all creation. The intent is to explore, honor, and revel in the majesty of God and be open to being astonished at Who He/She is in a fresh way. This is magnifying, reverential, and worshipful. As we do this we honor, include, and value ourselves and one another in a gloriously life-giving way - the way God intended.

So let's dive in!

CHAPTER ONE
GOD IN GENESIS, GOD BEFORE TIME

I remember in my "sneak reading" of the Bible when I was a little girl, I loved to read the Garden of Eden story in Genesis. What a wondrous and glorious existence that must have been (even if understood in allegorical terms)! How amazing to be perfect, innocent, naked, and unashamed in the Garden of Delight. In the Hebrew, *Eden* means "pleasure," which is so cool. God is definitely not a killjoy! If God is going to clear up confusion about masculinity and femininity and our relationship with one another, we need to go to the original design of our creation with fresh eyes.

So let's pause and ask God for fresh eyes and open hearts to what He/She wants to show us!

Papa/Jesus/Holy Spirit, thank You for Your kindness and Your goodness. Thank You that You always lead and guide us into all Truth. Thank You that You are safe and masterful. You heal our hearts and minds. You heal our eyes to see as You see. You heal our relationships with You, ourselves, and one another. You transform us into Your glorious image in our flavor from glory to glory. Help us see You, ourselves, and one another with clear, lovely, and fresh eyes! In Jesus' name, amen!

Clues about God in the Beginning

Clues about the maleness and femaleness of God can be found at the beginning in Genesis 1:1–5, which says:

> *¹ In the beginning **God (Elohim)** created [by forming from nothing] the heavens and the earth. ² The earth was formless and void or a waste and emptiness, and darkness was upon the face of the deep [primeval ocean that covered the unformed earth]. The **Spirit of God was moving (hovering, brooding)** over the face of the waters. ³ And God said, "Let there be light"; and there was light.*
>
> *The Amplified Bible* (emphasis mine)

"God" in Genesis 1:1 is the Hebrew word *elohiym*, which is a plural *masculine* noun. God is revealed here as masculine. This is not a surprise. In verse 2, however, the Spirit of God was moving (hovering, brooding) over the face of the waters. The word "Spirit" is the Hebrew word *ruwach*, which is a *feminine* noun. Moreover, the hovering and brooding activity is like the brooding female birds do over their chicks.

So far, we see the femaleness of Holy Spirit. Let's keep going.

Humanity, Male and Female, the Image and Likeness of God

Genesis 1:26–28 in the *New American Standard Bible* (*NASB*) says:

> *²⁶ Then God said, "Let Us make **mankind** in **Our image**, according to **Our likeness**; and let **them rule** over the fish of the sea and over the birds of the sky and over the livestock and over all the earth, and over every crawling thing that crawls on the earth." ²⁷ So God created **man in His own image**, in the image of God He created him; **male and female He created them**. ²⁸ God blessed **them**; and God said to **them**, "**Be fruitful and multiply, and fill the earth, and subdue it; and rule** over the fish of the sea and over the birds of the sky and over every living thing that moves on the earth."*

Here "man," "mankind," or "humankind" is the Hebrew word *adam*, which is a *male* noun. However, Adam was created male *and* female. Note, Adam was created male and female in the image and likeness of God. Stating it another way, the image and likeness of God could only be expressed in both femaleness *and* maleness in order to reflect that image.

God was not completely expressed in the male but required female expression, even if it was originally hidden. Hiddenness does not mean secondary in importance or value. After all, so much of the profoundness of God is hidden to be revealed.

I would also add that there is no evidence that Adam, before Eve was expressed, was morphing back and forth, in fluid fashion, between masculinity and femininity, nor that there was a hermaphroditic (having both male and female reproductive organs) amalgamation, the way we see in some primal plant and animal species. Indeed, God separated the feminine from the masculine because it was not good that Adam should be alone (Gen. 2:18–22).

Also note, the command to be fruitful and multiply and have rule and dominion was to both the man *and* the woman, and it was to be benevolently over everything *but* one another. There was no hierarchy between genders—neither man ruling over woman nor woman ruling over man. This is demonstrated by the Trinity (Father, Son, and Holy Spirit) as other-giving Love, submitting to one another, without hierarchy within the Godhead. This is one of the most astounding things about God—He submits, even to *our* will. He models what He tells us to do (Eph. 5:21 and 1 Pet. 5:5).

As we move along in our study, we will constantly see both male *and* female represented in the Godhead. Genesis 2:7 says:

> *⁷ Then **the Lord God** formed the **man** of dust from the ground, and breathed into **his** nostrils the breath of life; and the **man** became a living person.*
>
> *NASB* (emphasis mine)

"Lord God" is the Hebrew words *Yĕhovah 'elohiym*. We have seen that *elohiym* is a plural *male* noun. *Yĕhovah* is proper noun with reference to deity. Interestingly, this proper name of the one true God *does not reference* a gender.

Continuing in Genesis 2:7, we note the following:

> *⁷ Then the Lord God formed the man of dust from the ground,*

*and breathed into his nostrils the **breath of life**; and the man became a **living person**.*

NASB (emphasis mine)

The "breath of life" is the Hebrew word *Nĕshamah*, which is a *feminine* noun for "breath," "spirit of God," "man," and "every living thing." I purport this is yet another reference to Holy Spirit and is a feminine one.

Also note the word for "living person" is translated in other translations as "soul." It is the Hebrew word *nepēs*, and this is a *feminine* noun. Adam, who was male, was made alive as a feminine soul when Holy Spirit, referred to in a feminine way, breathed life into him.

A final verse to illuminate this discussion is Genesis 2:21–24, which says:

> *[21] So the Lord God caused a deep sleep to fall upon the man, and he slept; then He took one of his ribs and closed up the flesh at that place. [22] And the Lord God **fashioned into a woman** the rib which He had taken from the man, and brought her to the man. [23] Then the man said,*
> *"At last this is bone of my bones, And flesh of my flesh; She **shall be called 'woman,'** Because she was **taken out of man**."*
> *[24] For this reason **a man shall leave his father and his mother, and be joined to his wife; and they shall become one flesh**. [25] And the man and his wife were both **naked, but they were not ashamed**.*
>
> *NASB* (emphasis mine)

I have a few comments. The substance of Adam (the male with the female hidden), was fashioned into a woman (Hebrew: *'ishshah*). Interestingly, this fashioning is stated as the reason the male leaves his parents and cleaves to the female, becoming one flesh—back to original design. It is telling that the male leaves his parents to cleave, not the female leaving her parents to cleave. There's a lot to think about here.

Moving on, when they were separated, they were naked in masculinity and naked in femininity, and there was no shame. God's design for His kids is pre-approved, without spot or blemish before Him, chosen in Love (Eph. 1:4). There is no shame in the nakedness of either gender. Shaming one gender (i.e., the battle of the sexes), either female bashing or male bashing, is *not* okay. Both male and female stand before their Maker fully known, fully approved, fully equal, and fully adored—gorgeous!

See the beautiful, complementary interplay between the male and female? One is neither more preeminent nor valued more than the other. Each in their differences requires the other for completeness. Just as one member of the Godhead is neither more preeminent nor valued than the other, neither is the male or female expression more preeminent nor valued more than the other—so beautiful!

Hierarchy in the Godhead/Hierarchy in the Genders?

Let me take a moment to remind us how the orthodoxy of the church fathers/mothers has addressed the equality and lack of hierarchy within the Trinity. This seeming tangent is pertinent to our discussion if you will bear with me for a moment.

First, let me assert that the Son is not subordinate to the Father, nor to the Holy Spirit. The Nicene Creed, the bedrock of orthodoxy, states, "Lord Jesus Christ, the only Son of God, begotten from the Father before all ages, **God** from God, **Light** from Light, **true God** from true God, begotten, not made; **of the same essence** as the Father. Through him all things were made" (emphasis mine).

The heresy called Arianism stated that the Son is neither co-equal nor co-eternal with the Father, but is subordinate to God and of a changeable creature (the Son not being of the same substance as the

Father). Arianism was condemned by Arius's Bishop Alexander and in 325 at the Council of Nicaea.

Moreover, particularly pertinent to our discussion, Holy Spirit is neither subordinate to the Father nor the Son. The Nicene Creed also states that Holy Spirit shares the *same titles* as both the Father and the Son, being identified as "the Lord" (a title given to both the Father and the Son numerous times) and "the giver of life," a title that makes obvious allusions to creation, as do the Father and Son. Moreover, Holy Spirit shares in the honor and praise that is due to the other two members of the Trinity. The Spirit is to be worshiped along with them. In the same breath that you use to worship the Father and the Son, you worship the Spirit.

I am elaborating on orthodoxy at this time for a good reason. So far, we see that there is much more overt femaleness seen in the Person of Holy Spirit versus more hidden (but undeniable) femaleness in Father God and Jesus. I'll unpack more of this later.

If there are lurking perspectives that Holy Spirit is somehow less than in any way to the other members of the Trinity, that could justify viewing women as intrinsically less than, subordinate, ancillary, or secondary to men. *This* would actually be heretical, going counter to orthodoxy from church fathers and mothers, who were much closer to the incarnate Christ and the early church.

With this in mind, we will see repeated interplay between the feminine and masculine regarding God in all Members of the Trinity in His/Her attributes and modes of manifesting. This repeated interplay is both intricate and exquisitely beautiful.

God before Time, Male and Female

Let's go back *prior* to the Genesis account to John 1:1, which says:

> *¹ In the beginning was the **Word**, and the **Word** was with **God**, and the **Word** was **God**.*   *NASB* (emphasis mine)

"Word" in this scripture is the Greek word *Logos*, and it refers to Jesus. Not surprisingly, it is a *masculine* noun. "God" referenced here reflects Father God and is the Greek *theos*, another *masculine* noun. However, proceeding to John 1:4–5, we see another feminine reference:

> *⁴ **In Him** was **life**, and the **life** was the **Light** of men. ⁵ The **Light** shines in the darkness, and the darkness did not [b]comprehend it.*   *NASB* (emphasis mine)

The Greek word for "life" is the word *Zōē*, which is a *feminine* noun. The Greek word for "Light" is the word *phōs*, which is a *neuter noun*. The Greek word for "men" is the word *anthrōpos*, a *masculine* noun that refers to all human beings, whether male or female.

This means in Christ, definitely masculine, there is the feminine "life" and neuter "Light." Moreover, this female "life" is the neuter "Light" of the masculine "men."

Continuing to John 1:14, we find many feminine attributes to the masculine "Word" (referring to Christ):

> *¹⁴ And the **Word** became **flesh**, and dwelt among us; and we saw His **glory**, glory as of the only **Son** from the **Father**, full of **grace** and **truth**.*   *NASB* (emphasis mine)

Reviewing the Greek words for "flesh," "glory," "grace," and "truth," we find that they are ALL *feminine* nouns.[1]

---

1   The Greek word for "flesh" is *sarx*, a *feminine* noun. In a way, the *masculine* Word/Christ manifested in *feminine* flesh (which was sinless, by the way).
The Greek word for "glory" is *doxa*, a *feminine* noun.
The Greek word for "Son" is *Yhios*, a *masculine* noun—not a shocker. The Greek word for "Father" here is *patēr*, not surprisingly a *masculine* noun.
"Grace" is the Greek word *charis*, and it is a *feminine* noun.
Moreover, the Greek word for "truth" is *alētheia*, and is also a *feminine* noun.

The Greek for "Son" and "Father" are not surprisingly masculine nouns.

How rich is it that when the masculine "Word" (Jesus) became the feminine "flesh," He revealed His feminine "glory," full of the feminine "grace" and the feminine "truth"?

The inclusive nature of God for both men and woman is so beautifully and seamlessly revealed! God manifests in both the feminine and masculine. What a breathtaking God!

CHAPTER TWO

IN CHRIST MASCULINITY AND FEMININITY

Oneness—a God Concept

There is so much discussion of oneness in the body of Christ. I think that is wonderful. However, one of my pet peeves is when we gather in "unity services" to promote oneness around doctrinal agreement or "good feelings." Oneness of humanity is a right now reality in Christ, where there is union as well as distinction.

We were never called to homogeneousness. We were called to oneness with a vast array of unique expressions in line with the wholeness or holiness of Love Himself/Herself. This is what Jesus prayed for in John 17:20–23, saying that the glory He gave us would empower us to be one as He and His Father are one. This displays the truth that the Father sent the Son and loves all humanity as much as He loves Jesus. Now that is the high water mark of oneness!

Let's unpack this a bit more. Jesus prayed to His and our Father in John 17:20–23, which says:

> [20] *And I ask not only for these disciples, but also for all those who will one day believe in me through their message.* [21] *I pray for* ***them all to be joined together as one even as you and I, Father, are joined together as one****. I pray for them to become one with us so that the world will recognize that you sent me.* [22] *For the* ***very glory you have given to me I have given them so that they will be joined together as one and experience the same unity that we enjoy.*** [23] ***You live fully in me and now I live fully in them so that they will experience perfect unity****, and the world will be convinced that you have sent me, for they will see that* ***you love each one of them with the same passionate love that you have for me.*** *The Passion Translation* (emphasis mine)

In his commentary that accompanies this verse, Brian Simmons says about the "perfect unity" in verse 23 that the Aramaic definition is "shrink into one." When we see one another, our vaulted opinions of ourselves will shrink.

Where one gender sees themselves above the other in worth, value, or pre-eminence, there is a humility that needs be worked in.

And God is just the One to do it. God opposes the proud (who will eventually be humbled) and gives grace to the humble (James 4:6 and 1 Pet. 5:5). Too often as human beings, we take a come-uppance directive upon ourselves, which usually causes us to land in the opposite ditch. We go from male chauvinism to male bashing. And who loses? Everybody! Both ditches cause us to drown in toxic ditch water. When we belittle others, we belittle ourselves.

But God celebrates the uniqueness of masculinity and femininity. His truth of oneness is not sameness. We can be in unity with one another without losing the beauty and power of our distinct masculinity and femininity.

In the world, however, there is much blurring and confusion. In the business/professional world, women have felt the pressure to be more masculine. I remember when training as a physician, my femininity was often criticized and called into question—as if my ability to assimilate a differential diagnosis from history findings, physical exam results, and lab findings in order to come up with treatment options was somehow thwarted by my femininity. Instinctively, I refused to defeminize myself to meet some sort of artificial masculine standard. To tell the truth, I'm rather pleased about that. Though I had many other insecurities, on this front, I was solid. It must have been the grace of God! I strove to practice excellent medicine with a clean conscience before God.

On the flip side, there are many cultural dynamics that are feminizing men. This can be seen all too often in the church world. The fruit of the Spirit has been feminized so that with an overemphasis on gentleness, we forget that Love Himself in masculine form overturned tables in the name of Love. There's nothing wimpy about God in masculine expression. For that matter, there's nothing wimpy about God in feminine expression. God is not confused, but dang, we sure are!

The "gentle" fruit of the Spirit are oh so tender when required by Love. However, the same fruit can kick butt too! There's no need to take names; He/She has already called us by ours. Consider Proverbs

25:15, which says, *"Through patience a ruler may be persuaded, And a gentle tongue breaks bone"* (*NASB*).

Wow, I have to laugh! There is no need to feminize men or masculinize women to mediate justice, self-protect, or meet some confused standard that is not in line with truth.

The beautiful thing is that God reveals Himself/Herself as the gold standard of everything. He expresses Himself in masculinity that is solid, unchangeable, knowable, unyielding, and protective—like rock, a shield, and a tower. She expresses Herself as femininity that is flowing, graceful, mysterious, and receptive—like water and wind.

Both expressions are highly prized, neither one more than the other. We need both, and we *get* both. They are One! They are intermarried, as Christ is with His Bride—the three as One.

And so it is with humanity. We need *both* masculinity and femininity in all walks of life. There's a oneness with distinction that brings richness that we require.

Wow, there is so much here, I find myself leaping around inside like our old Jack Russel Terrier, Duke! I have to extend myself a loving "down girl."

Let's keep going!

Oneness, with Distinction

The truth of us being joined together—human to human and God to human, as tightly knit as Papa, Jesus, and Holy Spirit—holds the tension of right now truth that is manifesting, but has not fully manifested yet (Rom. 5:10, Eph. 1:4, Heb. 4:3, 2 Cor. 5:19, and Rev. 13:8). We are growing in our experience of this oneness more seamlessly as we engage with Them (Phil. 2:12; Rom. 12:2, 8:29). Scholarship involves the mind, but relationship involves the heart.

And happily, we get *everything*!

Paul alludes to oneness, as demonstrated by the Trinity, causing us to embrace the male and female, but not to overstate the distinction in Christ. I believe this mirrors maleness and femaleness within the Godhead, Who is One (Mark 12:29). Galatians 3:27–28 states:

> *^{27} Faith immersed you into Christ, and now you are covered and clothed with his life. ^{28} And we **no longer see each other in our former state**—Jew or non-Jew, rich or poor, **male or female**—because we're all one through our union with Jesus Christ.*
> TPT (emphasis mine)

This "not relating to one another" (except through our oneness in Christ) is also echoed by Christ in John 8:15, which says:

> *^{15} For you've set yourselves up as **judges of others based on outward appearances**, but I certainly **never** judge others in that way.* TPT (emphasis mine)

What all this means exactly is mysterious. Clearly, male and female are not interchangeable, and we don't ignore the differences. Indeed, God loves *healthy* diversity—*vive la différence!* Maleness and femaleness, as well as marriage between them, is enigmatic. This mystery of marriage is echoed in Mark 12:18 and 23–25, which says:

> *^{18} Some of the Sadducees, a religious group that denied there was a resurrection of the dead, came to ask Jesus this question:*
> *^{23} "So here's our dilemma: Which of the seven brothers will be the woman's husband when she's resurrected from the dead, since they all were once married to her?"*
> *^{24} Jesus answered them, "You are mistaken **because your hearts are not filled with the revelation** of the **Scriptures or the power of God**. ^{25} For when they **rise from the dead**, men and women will not marry, just like the angels of heaven don't marry.*
> TPT (emphasis mine)

Marriage and maleness/femaleness are, as the footnotes put it in Ephesians 5:31–32, a mega-mystery!

> *³¹ For this reason a man is to leave his father and his mother and lovingly hold to his wife, since the two have become joined as one flesh. ³² Marriage is the beautiful design of the Almighty, a great mystery of **Christ** and his **church**.*
> *TPT* (emphasis mine)

Jesus as the Christ is *male* and His church (Greek: *ekklēsia*), made up of male and female, is a *female* noun. Men are included not only as the feminine church, but as the feminine bride of Christ (Rev. 19:7; 21:2, 9; 22:17). Moreover, women are included as the masculine sons of God (Matt. 5:9; Rom. 8:14, 19; Gal 3:26, 4:6). How does all that work? God knows, but it is beautifully intriguing paradox!

Healing Humanity in Masculinity and Femininity

God is about the sweeping business of redeeming all things—drawing all things to Him/Herself![2] This makes such an astoundingly beautiful and powerful study that I referenced a bounty of scriptures to study and meditate upon below. Among what God is redeeming in us is the healing of masculinity and femininity in human form, including its effects on our identities, relationships, sexuality, marriages, and more. What this looks like is worthy of its own extensive series of books. But my mandate is to stay focused on God in masculine and feminine expression, which is the foundation—the cornerstone and the capstone of what healthy humanity in masculine and feminine expression looks like. I reverentially do not want to overstep.

---

2   Luke 3:5–6; 1 Cor. 15:26–28; 2 Cor. 5:17–19; Eph. 1:7–10, 19–23; Eph. 4:1; Phil. 2:9–1; Col. 1:19–20; Titus 2:11, 14; Heb. 2:8; Rev. 5:13, 7:9–10, and 21:4–5

I will say that God is conforming us into the image of Christ—God incarnating human flesh, including masculine and feminine flesh. That healing process embraces healthy, whole, and robust masculinity and femininity—without conflation or confusion—as expressed through each and every one of His/Her priceless kids. It also addresses the safety we need to embrace our bodies, our sexuality, and all things male and female.

I certainly don't have all the answers. But I am ever so grateful that the One Who *is* other-giving, self-sacrificial, co-suffering Love is faithful, able, and relentless in His/Her engaging with us in the healing process.

CHAPTER THREE
GETTING WISDOM

We are admonished repeatedly, almost to the point of obnoxiousness, to do anything it takes to get and keep to wisdom and understanding (Prov. 4:1, 5, and 7). Proverbs 4:5–9 puts it so beautifully:

> *⁵ So **make wisdom your quest**— search for the revelation of life's meaning. Don't let what I say go in one ear and out the other.*
> *⁶ **Stick with wisdom** and **she** will stick to you, protecting you throughout your days. **She** will rescue all those who passionately listen to **her** voice.*
> *⁷ **Wisdom is the most valuable commodity**—so buy it! Revelation-knowledge is what you need—so invest in it!*
> *⁸ **Wisdom will exalt you when you exalt her truth.** She will lead you to honor and favor when you live your life by her insights.*
> *⁹ **You will be adorned with beauty and grace,** and wisdom's glory will wrap itself around you, making you victorious in the race.* TPT (emphasis mine)

"Wisdom" (Hebrew: ḥāḵmâ) and "understanding" (Hebrew: bînâ) are both *feminine* nouns. They are personified as female, full of beauty and grace.

"Beauty" and "grace" in verse nine of this translation are literally "a garland of grace" and "a crown of beauty or glory." Teasing these apart, we find "garland," "crown," and "beauty" (or "glory") are *feminine* nouns, while "grace" here (as opposed to elsewhere) is surprisingly a *masculine* noun.[3]

So we see the feminine over and over, and this is not surprising, but it is rather refreshing.

I love the surprise of the masculine "grace" hidden in there. "Grace" here carries a flavor of favor, charm, elegance, and acceptance. This interchange of the feminine and the masculine is seen over and over,

---

3   "Garland" is the Hebrew word *livyâ*, a *feminine* noun.
"Grace" is the Hebrew word *ḥēn*, a *masculine* noun—this was a surprise!
"Crown" is the Hebrew word *ʿăṭārâ*, a *feminine* noun.
"Beauty" or "glory" is the Hebrew word *tipʾārâ*, a *feminine* noun.

even when one gender gets most of the attention. No one gender is ever forgotten or subsumed in the other. This is so reminiscent of Papa, Jesus, and Holy Spirit as other-giving Love, united but distinct, pointing to and reveling in One Another—no one Person above or below. We have so much to learn!

Wisdom as a Deity Personified as a Woman

Wisdom in both the Old and New Testaments is God (deity), not just an attribute, and is personified as a woman. Proverbs 1:19–21 reveals this quite clearly:

> [20] **Wisdom** shouts in the street,
> **She** raises **her** voice in the public square;
> [21] At the head of the noisy streets **she** cries out;
> At the entrance of the gates in the city **she** declares **her** sayings.
> NASB (emphasis mine)

"Wisdom" in this passage is the Hebrew word ḥākmâ, a *feminine* noun. Notice the repetitive use of "she" and "her."

Wisdom is also referred to in Isaiah 11:2, which is all about Jesus, the Christ, indisputably masculine. But Christ is described with overwhelmingly feminine Holy Spirit attributes:

> [2] The **Spirit** of the Lord will rest on **Him**,
> The **spirit** of **wisdom** and **understanding**,
> The **spirit** of **counsel** and **strength**,
> The **spirit** of **knowledge** and the **fear of the Lord**.
> NASB (emphasis mine)

Note, the Hebrew words for "Spirit," "Wisdom," "Understanding," "Counsel," "Strength" (this one surprised me, love curve balls), and "Fear of the Lord" are ALL *feminine* nouns. Wow! "Lord" in this passage is notably the *non-gendered* pronoun Yᵉhōvâ and "Knowledge" is both a *masculine* and *feminine* noun.⁴

Thus, Holy Spirit, in feminine expression, was resting upon Christ with all Her/His feminine attributes of:

- wisdom
- understanding
- counsel
- strength or might (the curve ball here)
- and fear of the Lord

Holy Spirit, in feminine expression, was resting upon Christ with Her/His dual male and feminine attribute of:

- knowledge

Christ (masculine) functions in union with the feminine Spirit and was empowered in the incarnation (here prophetically) by Her/His five feminine manifestations (one masculine).

Wisdom in the New Testament

What about wisdom in the New Testament? "Wisdom" in James 1:5 is the Greek word *sophia* and is also a *feminine* noun. It says:

> ⁵ *But if any of you lacks* **wisdom**, *let him ask of* **God**, *who gives to all generously and without reproach, and it will be given to him.*   NASB (emphasis mine)

---

4   Note, the repeated word "Spirit" here is once again the *feminine* Hebrew word *ruwach*.
"Wisdom" is the Hebrew word *ḥāḵmâ*, a *feminine* noun.
"Understanding" is the Hebrew word *bînâ*, another *feminine* noun.
"Counsel" is the Hebrew word *ʿēṣâ*, another *feminine* noun.
"Strength" or "might" is the Hebrew word *gᵉbûrâ*, yet another *feminine* noun.
"Knowledge" is the Hebrew word *daʿatl*, both a *masculine* and *feminine* noun.
"Fear of the Lord" is the Hebrew word *yirʾâ*, yet another *feminine* noun, with "Lord" notably being the *non-gendered* pronoun *Yᵉhōvâ*.

Note, "God" here is the Greek *masculine* noun *theos*. Thus, the masculine God gives the feminine wisdom generously.

This is reminiscent of when Christ asked the Father to send the Spirit. Holy Spirit has already been poured out upon all flesh, but we have an ongoing need to experience the fullness of Holy Spirit—the Spirit of Wisdom—already given to us. And that involves an engagement with the feminine.

In Ephesians 1:17–18, there is also an illuminating reference to wisdom. Here Paul prays:

> [17] *that the **God** of our **Lord Jesus Christ**, the **Father** of **glory**, may give you a **spirit** of **wisdom** and of **revelation** in the **knowledge** of **Him**.*
>
> *NASB* (emphasis mine)

Here's the cluster of *masculinity* in the Greek: "God," "Lord," and "Father."[5]

Here is the cluster of *femininity* in the Greek: "Glory," "Wisdom," "Revelation," and "Knowledge."[6]

The cluster of *neutral* (or both male and female) in the Greek is:

- "Spirit" is the Greek word *pneuma*, a *neuter* noun
- "Him" is the Greek word *autos*, a pronoun: he, she, it or himself, herself, themselves, itself

---

5   "God" is the Greek word *theos*, a *masculine* noun
"Lord" is the Greek word *kyrios*, a *masculine* noun.
Note, "Christ" is the Greek word *christos* (actually an adjective and a title).
"Father" is the Greek word *patēr*, a *masculine* noun.

6   "Glory" is the Greek word *doxa*, a *feminine* noun.
"Wisdom" is the Greek word *Sophia*, again, a *feminine* noun.
"Revelation" is the Greek word *apokalypsis*, a *feminine* noun.
"Knowledge" is the Greek word *epignōsis*, a *feminine* noun.

Apparently, the "Him" probably references Christ, but if it references God in general, Holy Spirit definitely has feminine overtones.

Ephesians 1:18 continues:

> *¹⁸ I pray that the **eyes of your heart** may be enlightened, so that you will know what is the **hope** of His **calling**, what are the **riches** of the **glory** of His inheritance in the saints.*
> *NASB* (emphasis mine)

The cluster of *femininity* in the Greek that Holy Spirit illuminates includes: "Eyes of your heart" (translated elsewhere as "understanding" or "imagination"), "Hope," "Calling," and "Glory."[7]

The reference to *masculinity* is "Riches," which is the Greek word *ploutos*, a *masculine* noun.

References that are *neutral* (or both male and female) in the Greek include:

- "His" is once again the Greek word *autos*, a pronoun: he, she, it or himself, herself, themselves, itself (see above)
- "Saints" is *hagios*, which is actually an adjective

Interestingly, in Ephesians 1:19, Holy Spirit enlightens our eyes to know the mighty power toward us. "Power" is the Greek word *dynamis* and is also a *feminine* noun—a big surprise as well.

What an astounding and illuminating survey! With the propensity of the female being illuminated in the midst of the masculine Father

---

7   "Eyes of your heart" (translated elsewhere as "understanding" or "imagination") is the Greek word *dianoia*, a *feminine* noun.
"Hope" is the Greek word *elpis*, a *feminine* noun.
"Calling" is the Greek word *klēsis*, a *feminine* noun.
"Glory" is the Greek word *doxa*, a *feminine* noun.

and Jesus, it is reminiscent of the hidden Eve being brought forth into the open or unveiled from Adam.

Apparently, God has a premium for expressing Him/Herself through the feminine and masculine—through His/Her daughters *as well as* His/Her sons!

All are exquisitely, intricately, and seamlessly represented!

CHAPTER FOUR

THE BATTLE OF THE SEXES AND GOD

I vividly remember being glued to my black and white television set (yes, there was such a thing) for the exhibition "battle of the sexes" tennis match played in 1973. This played out at the Houston Astrodome between 55-year-old Bobby Riggs and 29-year-old Billie Jean King. In the end, Billie Jean won in three sets.

I am not sure if Bobby Riggs was playing for the camera or for the $100,000 winner-take-all prize, but I remember him being shockingly cocky and rude to Billie, saying something about how women should be kept barefoot and pregnant. As a little girl, I cheered out loud when Billie Jean won! It seemed so apropos in light of the outrageous disrespect and condescension thrown at Billie, and inadvertently at women and girls in general.

The clash between genders, however, is not a recent phenomenon. Since the Fall, the consequences for choosing independence from God has resulted in incalculable fallout, including the battle of the sexes. And all is not fair in "lovelessness" and war!

Let's be clear: when God stated the "curses" (meaning consequences) that would befall men and women, He was *not* pronouncing them to punish them. He was stating the consequences of their deception and rebellion, and of the choice to operate from the delusion in their minds of being separated from God—catastrophic (Col. 1:21–22 and John 3:20–21)! The ramifications of the Fall resulting in bondage for women (and men) can be seen in Genesis 3:16, which says:

> *16 To the **woman** He said, "I will greatly multiply Your pain in childbirth, In pain you shall deliver children; Yet your **desire** will be for your **husband**, And he shall **rule over** you."*   *NASB* (emphasis mine)

The consequences that beset the woman were the beginning of the gender wars. The word "desire" is the Hebrew word *tᵉšûqâ*, which means "to desire to overcome or defeat"—literally "outstretch" in the Aramaic (not God's design).

Interestingly, the word "husband" was chosen in all of the English texts I found. It is the Hebrew word 'îš, which is most often translated as "man/men" and less frequently translated as "husband." Moreover, "woman" was used here in all the English texts I reviewed, not "wife" (both are the Hebrew word 'iššâ). This is counter to the concept of "man and wife," where a woman is defined in terms of her relationship with her husband, but her husband is a free agent so to speak.

I suspect these ramifications are greater than the dynamic of fallen marital relations and, while generalized to all relationships between men and women, are epitomized in marriage. No wonder Christ came in the flesh to, among other things, point to what His redeemed version of marriage is between Himself and His bride (Eph. 5:32).

The Hebrew word for "rule over" is *māšal*, which means to rule/reign over, have dominion (apart from God's design). God is saying that in Eve's desire to take the upper hand or control her husband, she, as the weaker vessel *physically*, would be put down by force if necessary. She would be dominated or ruled over.

The consequence that came about basically forecasted that women would lose the battle of the sexes, and history has born this out repeatedly. Men took dominion over women, right along with the animals and earth. We can see this when Adam named the woman Eve, just as he named the animals he was to have dominion over (Gen. 2:20 and 3:20).

In a very real sense, what you name, you define. This subjugation and oppression was something outside the heart and expressed will of God (Gen. 1:26–28). Adam and Eve were given dominion over everything *but* one another. Women were never designed to be secondary in value or function, but they too often have been viewed and treated as such, covertly if not overtly. (Gen. 2:19–20; 3:20; 7:1, 7).

Let's be clear: women also have not been blameless, too often resorting to manipulation, control, or passive-aggression (sexually, emotionally, or otherwise) in order to try to gain the upper hand over men (*tᵊšûqâ*—"outstretching desire for the upper hand"*)*. They have emasculated or downright castrated men while complaining about men not being manly.

Having roughly an equal number of men and women as coaching clients, I have heard way too many horrible stories of the abuses of men at the hands of women. While the advent of the Me Too movement, where women have justly decried sexual exploitation at the hands of men, is an all-too-real thing, honorable men who have been falsely accused of sexual misconduct with the current "guilty until proven innocent" undercurrent have gone through hell as well. I can't help but have compassion for Rowlf the Dog and Kermit the Frog in their song of lamentation (*I Hope that Somethin' Better Comes Along*) over the high-maintenance Miss Piggy:

> [8]*You can't live with 'em. You can't live without 'em. There's something irresistible-ish about 'em. We grin and bear it 'cause the nights are long. I hope that something better comes along!*

Keep in mind, however, with the consequences of the Fall, women's greatest pain point would be that of childbirth and relations with men. Fallen ways of being for women more often fall along the lines of manipulation, control, and competing for men. This is turning away from God as their Source towards men who will inevitably fail them grievously. Men make lousy gods (as do women).

With the consequences of the Fall, men's greatest pain point would be the ground that, despite agonizing, sweaty toil, yields thorns and thistles (Gen 3:16–19). The turning of men away from God as their Source to the ground has led to the turf wars we see.

Whether it is defending your online domain, your client list, ousting the competition, or defending or challenging our national lines of

---

[8] Produced By Jim Henson & Paul Williams; Written By Kenneth Ascher & Paul Williams; Performed By Jim Henson; Release Date 1979

sovereignty, fighting over territory is a gigantic human (predominantly male) issue.

Violence and war ensue for the sake of turf. Part of that turf all too often is women. Even animals, usually male, mark their territory with their scent. They brutally duke it out to win rights to and over the female. Men brand cattle, sue one another for stealing intellectual property, initiate wars, oust governments, traffic women and children... mine, mine, mine, mine, mine! And meanwhile, the earth groans under the weight of the Fall, waiting for humanity to get a gigantic clue about who they are (Rom. 8:19–22).

All of this is a product of the Fall. What a mess! We desperately need a Savior. Thank God we have such a merciful, kind, and *masterful* One!

Because the vast majority of societies have been, and still are, to varying degrees insidiously or overtly patriarchal, this seeps into how humanity sees God and even how the Bible is translated. Even in our *enlightened* western culture, the long fight for equal pay for equal work was not over with the passage of the first Equal Pay legislation in 1970. What this act highlighted is that which has been apparent throughout the history of women's paid employment in the 19th and 20th centuries—namely that the real cause of women's low and unequal pay is the issue of job segregation and the consequential *undervaluing of women's skills*.

While women are seen in so many of what used to be male-dominated arenas, they are disproportionally underrepresented, if represented at all, in the upper echelons of those disciplines. This turf is jealously graded, and one of the greatest bastions of this is the church world itself.

I remember hearing one amazing male minister, who has written powerful books championing women, tell all the women at a conference to feel the top of their heads. "That bump you feel," he said, "is the glass ceiling you keep butting up against." A lump rose up in my throat to hear the beauty of the acknowledgement of a very real, relentless pain point! It meant so much that a man I respected would recognize that dynamic. However, he suddenly got very defensive and stated that *he* couldn't invite women to lead at his level at his church because that would mean he would have to step aside to make room. He quipped with a contentious tone that if you, as a woman, did come and minister, "you'd better be good."

How insulting! I felt like I was slapped in the face. I wanted to shout out, "You mean can't *share your turf* with a woman? And *if* you do, they'd *really* need to prove themselves? I guess there's not enough to go around, and a call from God needs to run through male approval. Bummer for the women." Clearly, even in our enlightenment, we have a ways to go.

When I matriculated into medical school at a prestigious Ivy League school, our class was, in fact, the first with more women than men. This was notable. However, the upper echelons of that school were and still are *markedly*, disproportionally male. I can remember maybe only one or two women on staff during my time there.

We see this in pretty much all seven mountains of influence, and arguably nowhere more so than in the church. Some of this phenomenon is, in all fairness, due to women's personal choice to bear and raise children, which has phenomenal (though more intangible) rewards. However, even taking this into account, there are still a lot of unanswered questions as to why a wage and representation gap exists.[9]

As I inferred previously, the bias and propensity to favor the male over the female can be seen in particularly ugly ways in the church. If we allow (and especially *require*) ourselves to be honest, it has even seeped into one Bible translation after another.

---

9   https://www.vox.com/2018/2/19/17018380/gender-wage-gap-child-care-penalty

Classic examples, and there are many beyond the scope of this work, include how we have *interpreted* scriptural dynamics between men and women:

- Women should learn in *quietness* and *full submission* and *not* teach or have authority over a man because Eve was *deceived* (1 Tim. 2:11-14)
- Women as the *weaker vessel* (1 Pet. 3:6-7)
- Women *should remain silent in the churches* (1 Cor. 14:34-35)

My experience in ministry, even freshly up to two weeks ago of my writing this, reveals that this area of attack is alive and viciously unwell. Some notable labels I have recently received are false teacher, false prophet (because, God forbid, I was a woman teaching outside of children's church and women's ministry), heretic, and my personal favorite, "daughter of satan". Sit down, shut up, and wear a doily on your head!

If the scriptures above are troubling for you, I recommend Jonathan Welton's chapter "Women Rising" in his excellent book [10]*Normal Christianity*. It will be a rigorous but gorgeous eye-opener!

I have run into myriads of women and have experienced for myself how devastating it can be when it feels like there is not only the pain of male domination and female victimization/minimization/peripheralization, but that God must have ordained it or at least be okay with it since *He* is male. It is such freedom for so many women who have felt and (let's be honest) have often been treated like objects, refuse, adornments, second-class citizens, or afterthoughts to know how God represents them in such a relentlessly sweeping way.

Moreover, it is freedom for men (I love the win-win. How *refreshing!*) to be supported and covered by women—not manipulated, controlled, nor minimized in areas of weakness. We are truly better together, championing one another as originally designed!

---

10   Welton, Jonathan. *Normal Christianity*. Destiny Image Publishers © copyright 2011

Surprising Twists

With all the very real battle of the sexes, I want to take a moment to edify the men as well with some surprising and powerful words that we have traditionally associated with women.

Did you know the Hebrew word *ēzer*, which was the word for "helpmeet" referring to Eve, is actually a *masculine* noun (Gen. 2:18)? I had to triple check that, but yes! The expression of Eve from Adam was *feminine*. She was later named Eve, "mother of all living things" (Gen. 3:20). But she also carried the *masculine* as a help-meet. What a surprise and mystery—so lovely!

Moreover, the Greek word for "Helper/Comforter" is the word *Paraklētos*, which one tends to think of as feminine, but which is actually a *masculine* noun. John 14:16–17 says:

> [16] *And I will ask the Father, and He will give you another* **Helper (Comforter, Advocate, Intercessor—Counselor, Strengthener, Standby)**, *to be with you forever—* [17] *the Spirit of Truth, whom the world cannot receive [and take to its heart] because it does not see* **Him** *or know* **Him**, *but you know* **Him** *because* **He (the Holy Spirit)** *remains with you continually and will be in you.*
>
> AMP (emphasis mine)

Note the masculine verbiage here. So Holy Spirit is represented in both masculine and feminine terms throughout scripture. Holy Spirit is also referred to in gender neutral terms in Matthew 3:16–17, which says:

> [16] *After He was baptized, Jesus came up immediately from the water; and behold, the heavens were opened, and* **he** *saw the* **Spirit** *of* **God** *descending as a* **dove** *and settling on Him,* [17] *and behold, a voice from the heavens said, "This is My beloved* **Son***, with whom I am well pleased."* NASB (emphasis mine)

The word "Spirit" is the Greek word *pneuma*, which is a *neuter* noun. "God" here is the Greek word *theos*, which is *masculine*. However, the "Spirit of God" descends as a "dove." This is the Greek word *peristera*, which is a *feminine* noun.

Here again is a gorgeous interplay of the Trinity—the Son and Father (Who are masculine) and the Spirit (Who is neutral here) presenting as the feminine dove—fascinating!

God Is, Jesus Is

Let's turn our focus to Who God says He/She is. First John 4:8 in the *New American Standard Bible* states that *"The one who does not love does not know **God**, because **God** is **love**"* (emphasis mine).

The word for "God" is the Greek word *theos*, which is a *masculine* noun.

The word for "love" is the Greek word *agape*, which is a *feminine* noun.

Once again, the masculine God is expressed as the feminine Love! Interestingly, God *is* Love (feminine, *agape)* and does *not just express* the attribute of love. The masculine God is feminine. This is such a glorious enigma.

Here is not the only place this dynamic occurs. We see it throughout the seven *"I AM"* statements Jesus made in the book of John.

John 14:6 says, *"Jesus answered, 'I am the **way and the truth and the life**. No one comes to the Father except through me'"* (*NIV*, emphasis mine).
Jesus (masculine) says that He is the *way*, *truth*, and *life*.

"Way," "truth," and "life" are all *feminine* nouns in the Greek.[11] Jesus is masculine and, in very real terms, expresses Himself as feminine, unapologetically saying He IS, as the I AM, feminine.

John 10:7 says, *"Then Jesus said to them again, 'Most assuredly, I say to you, I am the **door** of the sheep'"* (New King James Version, emphasis mine).

Jesus is the "door" (the Greek word *thyra*), once again a *feminine* noun.
Incidentally, "sheep" is the Greek word *probation*, which is *gender neutral*. Everyone is equally included. I love that about God!

When Jesus says He is **"the bread of life"** (John 6:35), "bread" is the *masculine* Greek noun *artos*, and once again "life" is the *feminine* Greek noun *zōē*. Jesus (masculine) is masculine and feminine.

Jesus proclaims He is **"the resurrection and the life"** in John 11:25. Here, again:

- "Resurrection" is the *feminine* Greek noun *anastasis*
- "Life" is the *feminine* Greek noun *zōē*

Jesus (masculine) is expressed in feminine terms twice here.

When Jesus says He is **"the light of the world"** (John 8:12), "light" is the Greek noun *phōs* and is *gender neutral*.

When Jesus says He is **"the Good Shepherd"** (John 10:11), "Good Shepherd" is the Greek noun *poimēn*, which is a *masculine* noun.

When Jesus says He is **"the True Vine"** (John 15:1), "True Vine" is the Greek noun *alēthinos* and is *feminine*.

---

11   "Way" is the Greek word *hodos*, a *feminine* noun
"Truth" is the Greek word *alētheia*, a *feminine* noun.
"Life" is the Greek word *zōē*, a *feminine* noun.

So let's tally things. Out of the *God is Love* proclamation and seven "*I AM*" statements, the masculine Son of God made:

- Eight references to His I-AM-ness are *feminine*:
    o Love
    o Way
    o Truth
    o Life
    o Door
    o Resurrection
    o Light
    o True Vine
- One is *masculine* with a *feminine* component:
    o Bread of Life
- One is *masculine*:
    o Good Shepherd
- One is *gender neutral*:
    o Light

Wow! Apparently, God is very secure in His/Her masculinity and femininity. This is soooo good considering that humanity is so confused and insecure about it!

More Fun Insights

In the last section I discussed Jesus as "the life" (John 11:25). We see in 1 John 3:14 the contrast between death and life:

> *14 We know that we have passed out of **death** into **life**, because we love the brothers and sisters. The one who does not love remains in **death**.*   *NASB* (emphasis mine)

"Death" is the Greek *thanatos* and is a *masculine* noun.
"Life", once again, is the Greek *zōē* and is a *feminine* noun.
So, "God" (*masculine*) as Love (*feminine*) responds to the *masculine* death with the *feminine* life.

We also find the interplay between the masculine and feminine with the issue of sin and death in Romans 5:12 which says:

> *¹² Therefore, just as through **one man sin** entered into the world, and **death** through **sin**, and so **death** spread to all **mankind**, because all sinned—*
>
> NASB (emphasis mine)

"Man" and "mankind" are both the Greek *anthrōpos*, a *masculine* noun. "One man" refers to the first Adam, though the use of "mankind" includes both the masculine and feminine.
"Sin" is the Greek *hamartia*, a *feminine* noun.
"Death", once again, is the Greek *thanatos* and is a *masculine* noun.

Thus, we find that through the *masculine* first Adam, *feminine* sin entered into the world. Through the *feminine* sin, the *masculine* death spread to all the cosmos. There is culpability for both the masculine and feminine AND, as we shall happily see, salvation and redemption moves through both the masculine and feminine. How masterful is God!?

Another fun scripture to study is Romans 1:16, which says:

> *¹⁶ For I am not ashamed of the **gospel**, for it is the **power** of **God** for **salvation** to everyone who believes, to the Jew first and also to the Greek.*
>
> NASB (emphasis mine)

The word for "gospel" is the Greek word *euangelion*, which is a *neuter* noun. I love that! The gospel is for *all*, without reference to any one gender over another!

Interestingly, the word for "power" here is the Greek word *dynamis*, which is a *feminine* noun. This really was surprising! Moreover, the word *exousia*, usually translated as "authority" (Rom. 13:1), is also a *feminine* noun. Another surprise, since women have traditionally deferred/been made to defer to men who have generally asserted themselves to be the higher authority in matters outside the home.

"God" in Romans 1:16 is, once again, the *masculine* Greek word *theos*.

The word for "salvation" is the Greek word *sōtēria*, a *feminine* noun. Note, the word for "salvation" (i.e. Psalm 18:46*)* in the Hebrew is *yēša*, which is a *male* noun. We see both the male and female—yes, salvation is inclusive for *all!* Once again, the interplay of the masculine and feminine in the Godhead and what He/She expresses is truly amazing, and we see it over and over and over—intricate, beautiful, majestic, and mysterious!

CHAPTER FIVE

FEMININE EXPRESSIONS OF THE MASCULINE

There is nothing quite so touching as a solidly masculine father taking care of his children. Husbands, if you want to make your wife fall in love with you, be you, in your masculine strength *tenderly*, taking care of your kids or grandkids—a total turn on (hint, hint)!

Feminine Expressions of the Masculine in the Old Testament:

If you have been in the Christian community for a while, you no doubt have heard of Jehovah God as El Shaddai. This referral to God occurs seven times (the number of perfection and completion) and is most often believed to be derived from *shad*, meaning "breast" in Hebrew. Some other scholars believe that the name is derived from an Akkadian word *Šadu*, meaning "mountain," suggesting strength and power. Let me add that a mountain can also suggest the anatomy of the female breast. Note the Grand Teton Mountain range—"Teton" is French for "breast." Also, in the context of the verses in which it is used, it is more about provision (Gen. 17:1). A God of *many breasts* completely nourishes, satisfies, and supplies His/Her people with all of their needs as a mother would her child. And God has no "supply chain" issues—can I get an amen?!

Any mother who has breastfed knows that milk in the breasts is present but often waiting to be released at the cry of her child. I can relate, as when I was doing my first mother/baby portraits, my firstborn started crying. The released breast milk stained my outfit, and I had to reschedule. That may be too much information for some of you, but mothers who have experienced breastfeeding will smile and relate. How tender and motherly it is that God nourishes, provides, and sustains us in such an intimate, bonded way *at our cry*.

Note, the following are descriptions of Jehovah, Who most feel represents the Son (although the three members of the Godhead are always present). In Judaism, God was monotheistic, with the three

Persons of the Trinity present but veiled. Jehovah is masculine, but He presents in feminine terms!

An amazing case in point is Isaiah 49:14–16:

> *¹⁴ But Zion said, "The **Lord** has forsaken me, the **Lord** has forgotten me."*
> *¹⁵ "Can a **mother forget the baby at her breast** and have no compassion on **the child she has borne**?*
> *Though she may forget, I will not forget you!*
> *¹⁶ See, I have engraved you on the palms of my hands; your walls are ever before me."*
> NIV (emphasis mine)

You are so precious to God, Who shares in the bond of a baby born from the womb and an infant at the breast, that He/She has metaphorically engraved you on His/Her hands. A permanent mark *you* have made on Him/Her! You are so ever-present on His/Her mind and heart!

Another pertinent verse is Hosea 11:1–4, which also refers to Jehovah:

> *¹ "When Israel was a **child**, **I loved** him, and out of Egypt I called my son.*
> *² But the more they were called, the more they went away from me. They sacrificed to the Baals and they burned incense to images.*
> *³ **It was I who taught Ephraim to walk, taking them by the arms;** but they did not realize it was **I who healed them**.*
> *⁴ **I led them with cords of human kindness, with ties of love.** To them I was like **one who lifts a little child to the cheek, and I bent down to feed them.***   NIV (emphasis mine)

Savor the beautifully tender, *feminine* ministry of the Jehovah. Who most often teaches the toddler how to walk, taking them by the arms? Most often a mother. Who leads with cords of human kindness and ties of love (reminiscent of the umbilical cord)? Most often a mother. Who most often is the one who lifts a little child to their cheek and bends down to feed them? Most often a mother. Here truly is the mother heart of God!

Ezekiel 16:4, 6–8, 9–11, and 13–14 add to the picture of the maternal and paternal aspects of Jehovah. Scan the words in bold and let them paint you a picture.

> *[4] As for your **birth**, on the day you were born your **navel cord was not cut**, nor were you **washed with water for cleansing**; you were not rubbed with salt or even **wrapped in cloths**.*
> *[6] "When I **passed by you** and saw you squirming in your blood, I said to you while you were in your blood, '**Live!**' Yes, I said to you while you were in your blood, 'Live!' [7] I made you very numerous, like plants of the field. Then you **grew up**, became tall and reached the age for fine jewelry; your breasts were formed and your hair had grown. Yet you were naked and bare.*
> *[8] "Then I passed by you and saw you, and behold, you were at the time for love; so I **spread My garment over you** and covered your nakedness. I also swore an oath to you and entered into a covenant with you so that you became Mine," declares the Lord God. [9] "Then I **bathed you** with **water, washed off your blood from you, and anointed you with oil**. [10] I also **clothed you** with colorfully woven cloth and **put sandals of fine leather on your feet**; and I **wrapped you** with fine linen and **covered you with silk**. [11] I **adorned you** with jewelry, put bracelets on your wrists, and a necklace around your neck.*
> *[13] So you were adorned with gold and silver, and your **dress was of fine linen, silk**, and colorfully woven cloth. You **ate fine flour, honey, and oil**; so you were exceedingly beautiful and advanced to royalty. [14] Then your fame spread among the nations on account of your **beauty**, for it was **perfect** because of My **splendor which I bestowed on you**," declares the Lord God.*
> *NASB* (emphasis mine)

Just scanning the words in bold paints the beautiful, nurturing tenderness of the mother heart of God. This is seamlessly juxtaposed with the provisional, protective aspects of the father heart of God. God is a master parent!

Isaiah 66:9–13 also portrays another poetic picture of the feminine heart of God (Jehovah):

> *⁹ Do I bring to the **moment of birth and not give delivery?"** says the Lord. "Do I close up the womb when I **bring to delivery?"** says your God.*
> *¹⁰ "Rejoice with Jerusalem and be glad for her, all you who love her; rejoice greatly with her, all you who mourn over her.*
> *¹¹ For you will **nurse and be satisfied at her comforting breasts;***
> *you will drink deeply and delight in her overflowing abundance."*
> *¹² For this is what the Lord says: "I will extend peace to her like a river, and the wealth of nations like a flooding stream; **you will nurse and be carried on her arm and dandled on her knees.***
> *¹³ **As a mother comforts her child, so will I comfort you;** and you will be comforted over Jerusalem." NIV* (emphasis mine)

Once again, this is such nurturing, *maternal* imagery for the masculine Jehovah!

A final surprising example of this is in the sweeping pre-creation passage of Proverbs 8:22–31. The entire chapter is about Wisdom. In this passage, we find Wisdom (as the Person of Christ) co-creating with *Yᵉhōvâ* before time.

Proverbs 8:22–25 and 30–31 says:

> **Wisdom in the Beginning**
> *²² In the beginning I was there, for God possessed me even before he created the universe.*
> *²³ From eternity past I was set in place, before the world began.*

> *I was **anointed from the beginning.***
> ²⁴*Before the oceans depths were poured out, and before there were any glorious fountains overflowing with water, I was there, dancing!*
> ²⁵*Even before one mountain had been sculpted or one hill raised up, I was already there, dancing!*
> ³⁰*I was there, **close to the Creator's side as his master artist.** Daily he was filled with delight in me as I playfully rejoiced before him.*
> ³¹*I laughed and played, so happy with what he had made, while finding my delight in the children of men.* TPT (emphasis mine)

Brian Simmons comments, "What a beautiful picture we find here of Wisdom (Christ), who finds his fulfillment in us."

Interestingly, Wisdom here is a personification of God as Christ (Is. 11:2, John 1:1–3, and Heb. 1:2). However, Wisdom, as we have seen previously, is the Hebrew word ḥāḵmâ, a *feminine* noun. It is an astounding mystery of how the masculine Christ carries femininity. But this makes sense considering He died for *all* humanity—masculine and feminine.

Feminine Expressions of the Masculine in the New Testament:

Let's look at the Son, Jesus the Christ, as He presents in beautiful, feminine terms in the New Testament.

Matthew 23:37 states:

> ³⁷ *O Jerusalem, Jerusalem, thou that killest the prophets, and stonest them which are sent unto thee, how often would I have gathered thy children together, even as **a hen gathereth her***

chickens under her wings, and ye would not! KJV (emphasis mine)

The imagery here is a feminine one—a hen who gathers her chicks under her wings to protect, comfort, and nurture them! Study the following image.... How does it make you feel?

How safe and nurtured are you under God's strong but tender wings? I love the fact in this picture that the chicks are black, "white", and one that I can barely make out but that looks in-between. No one is outside of God's nurturing and protective covering![12] Can you imagine if something tried to mess with this mama hen's chicks?! Don't mess with God's kids (and psst, we're *all* God's kids)!

More feminine imagery connected with Christ is found in John 19:33–34, which says:

> [33] *but after they came to Jesus, when they saw that He was already dead, they did not break His legs.* [34] *Yet one of the*

---

12 Photography credit: https://silkie.org/do-chickens-nurse-their-young.html

*soldiers **pierced His side with a spear, and immediately blood and water came out.*** *NASB* (emphasis mine)

This is imagery of Christ *birthing* the church—a female bride—from His side. The second Adam, Christ, birthing the feminine church from His side mirrors the birth of the first woman, Eve, from the first Adam's side. Birthing is powerful, female imagery.

Jesus Elevating Women

Another pertinent discussion is Jesus relating the parables about the kingdom in Luke 15. He presents three parables about God pursuing His/Her lost kids. The first one is Luke 15:3–7 and is about a Good Shepherd (masculine), identified as the Son in John 10:11, pursuing His lost sheep (gender neutral). The last one is the Father (obviously masculine), with His open heart receiving the returning prodigal son and pursuing the legalistic elder brother (Luke 15:11–32). So we see the Son and Father in allegory pursuing Their lost kids. Sandwiched in-between these two parables is Luke 15:8–10, which says:

> *⁸Jesus gave them another parable: "There once was a **woman** who had ten valuable silver coins. When **she** lost one of them, **she** swept **her** entire house, diligently searching every nook and cranny for that one lost coin. ⁹When **she** finally found it, **she** gathered all **her** friends and neighbors for a celebration, telling them, 'Come and celebrate with me! I had lost my precious silver coin, but now I've found it.' ¹⁰**That's the way God responds** every time one lost sinner repents and turns to him. He says to all his angels, 'Let's have a joyous celebration, for the one who was lost, I have found!'"*
>
> *TPT* (emphasis mine)

Here we have a woman pursuing the precious single coin—allegorical for God's pursuit of His/Her lost children. The way this woman responds, we are told, is the way *God* responds. God responds in a female way. Even more pertinent is that the female woman pursuing lost kids is represented right alongside the Father and Son. "Woman" is the feminine Greek noun *gynē* and means "a woman of any age, whether a virgin, married, or widow, or a wife." To be exact: the "shes" used here are actually verbs, and "her" is not included in the original text. I don't think this woman is deified, but I do think it is pertinent that Jesus apparently had no problem saying that God rejoices just like the woman does over a sinner who repents. Moreover, Jesus pointedly didn't choose a man to search for a lost coin in this story, He *specifically* chose a woman. This honors women, putting them in the same function, allegorically, as the Father and Son.

How utterly revolutionary, considering Jesus was speaking to a society that considered and treated women not just as second class, but as possessions and as those deserving the blame for the Fall. The Jewish culture at the time was incredibly oppressive to women. In-between the time of the Mosaic law through Malachi and the New Testament Gospels (the silent years), Judaism increased the Levitical laws, adding to the original Ten Commandments, from 212 to 617 laws. They added roughly 400 more laws, and the Pharisee and Sadducee sects were born. Almost 100 of those additional 400 laws disempowered women.

In first-century Judaism, women were akin to slaves. They had no rights, no respect, and no voice. They were the property of men. They were allowed little or no formal education. Jewish women were forbidden to speak to men in public and had to veil their faces when they left the house. If a woman was caught unveiled in public, it was grounds for divorce. If a man came over to the house, the woman had to eat in another room. Their marriages were arranged by their fathers, and their husbands were allowed to marry *many* wives. If their husbands were tired or displeased with a wife, they could divorce them, discarding them like used rags. However, wives could not divorce their husbands.

Jewish women could not vote and could not even testify in court (they were believed to be inherent liars). They were relegated to the outer court (of five courts) of the synagogue. They were most often not allowed to read the Torah, and it was illegal for them to be taught scripture. Rabbi Eliezer, a first-century teacher, is noted for saying, "Rather should the word of the Torah be burned than entrusted to a woman." Women were not allowed to recite the morning prayer, nor prayers at meals. This is the culture in which Jesus moved.[13]

In Luke 15:3–32, Jesus gave these parables in the presence of scribes and Pharisees (*Pharisee* meaning "Separatist") as He was reaching out to sinners and tax collectors. Convicting the leaders about devaluing sinners and tax collectors drew them up short, but to elevate women, inferring that God is like a woman who searches for lost treasure, was nothing less than scandalous! After all, they did not believe that women were even created in the image of God like men were, and they blamed women for the Fall (as has much of the church, traditionally and to this day).

I always am amused—or (full-disclosure) ticked off, depending upon how charitable I am feeling (Love is still relentlessly conforming me to His/Her image)—at the historical prevalence of Eve being condemned for the Fall. Scripture says that Eve was deceived and Adam sinned (2 Cor. 11:3 and 1 Tim. 2:14). For Adam to transgress at the urging of the deceived woman, he was either a total wuss, or he was in flat-out rebellion against God. It was such a more foundational sin that it was necessary to incarnate Christ as the second *Adam* (not the second Eve) to overcome the calamity of the First *Adam* (not first Eve)—a thoughtful aside.

To sum up Luke 15:8–10, the pointed use of a woman in such a divine context in the parable, when Jesus was speaking to a highly patriarchal society, highlights the radical gender-inclusive nature of God and Him/Her functioning in both masculine and feminine expressions.

---

13   https://www.franciscanmedia.org/st-anthony-messenger/jesus-extraordinary-treatment-of-women

Holy Spirit's Female Representation in the New Testament

Let's talk about Holy Spirit in the New Testament for a bit. I discussed previously that Holy Spirit in John 14:26 is titled in *masculine* terms. The words "Comforter" or "Helper" are both the Greek word *paraklētos*, which is *masculine*.

> *²⁶ But the **Comforter** (Counselor, Helper, Intercessor, Advocate, Strengthener, Standby), the **Holy Spirit**, Whom the Father will send in My name [in My place, to represent Me and act on My behalf], **He** will teach you all things. And **He** will cause you to recall (will remind you of, bring to your remembrance) everything I have told you.* AMP (emphasis mine)

"Comforter" and "Helper" may be *masculine* nouns; however, "Holy Spirit" is the Greek word *pneuma*, which is *gender neutral*. He/She functions in very feminine ways—comforting, teaching, and nurturing.

Other insights include titles for Holy Spirit: "Spirit of Grace" is found in Hebrews 10:29. Here the *gender neutral* Greek word for "Spirit" (*pneuma*) is expressed in the *feminine* Greek word for "Grace" (*charis*). Once again, there is a leaning toward the *feminine*.

Another title for Holy Spirit is "Spirit of Truth," which I will address in this next section.

Gender Bias in Scripture?

One thing I love about the Bible is that is whitewashes nothing. It is life when, even in the ugly parts, we are supernaturally empowered to see it pointing to Christ and Trinity's finished work, if even in a hidden way. However, scripture, as inspired as it is, has been translated by humans (and let's say honestly, by men—little wiggle room here). These men were moved by Holy Spirit (2 Pet. 1:20–21), but they also inherently came with filters and biases, just like we *all* do. In their receiving/translating, they had to choose one word/phrase over others, according to their understanding. With this, filters and biases can be seen all too often. All of us need vast help and ongoing humility; we are utterly dependent upon the Word Himself in us to help us rightly interpret scripture, as well as prophetic encounters/dreams. He is the One to illuminate, convict, and heal us of our filters and biases.

Let's look at this phenomenon in John 14:17, which says:

> *17 Even the **Spirit of truth**; whom the world cannot receive, because it seeth **him** not, neither knoweth **him**: but ye know **him**; for **he** dwelleth with you, and shall be in you.*
> King James Version (emphasis mine)

"Spirit of truth" here is the *gender neutral* Greek word for "Spirit" (*pneuma*) and the *feminine* Greek word for "truth" (*alētheia*).

Interestingly, "Spirit of truth" is not only used in John 14:17, but also in John 15:26 and 16:13, using the same *gender neutral* Greek for "Spirit" and *feminine* Greek word for "truth." However, in all three scriptures, Holy Spirit is referred to as "he/him." The male pronouns "him" and "he" are the Greek words:

> **him**—*Autos,* used both times, is a pronoun without reference to gender and is translated: himself, *herself*, themselves, itself, or he, *she*, it.
> **he**—In this verse, *he* is actually not in the Greek, but it was added probably for clarity and flow. However, adding it magnifies the male bias issues at hand.

It was the *choice of the translator* to translate him/he, even though the Greek for "Spirit" is gender neutral and "Truth" is feminine. That is presumptuous at best and a frank bias at worst.

John 15:26 also alludes to the "Spirit of Truth" and says:

> ^{26} *But when the **Comforter** is come, whom I will send unto you from the Father, even the **Spirit of truth**, which proceedeth from the Father, **he** shall testify of me.* . . .
>
> KJV (emphasis mine)

Once again, "Comforter" is the *male* Greek noun *paraklētos*. "Spirit of Truth" is the *gender neutral* Greek noun for "Spirit," *pneuma*, paired with the *female* Greek noun for "truth," *alētheia*. So far, Holy Spirit is represented here as masculine, neutral, and feminine.

The word "he" is the Greek word *ekeinos*, which is a pronoun without reference to gender and is translated: he, *she*, it, etc. So once again, the bias is to refer to Holy Spirit in the male context only.

Let's see how John 16:13 paints Holy Spirit:

> ^{13} *Howbeit when **he**, the **Spirit of truth**, is come, **he** will guide you into all truth: for **he** shall not speak of **himself**; but whatsoever **he** shall hear, that shall **he** speak: and **he** will shew you things to come.*
>
> KJV (emphasis mine)

Once again, "Spirit of truth" is the *gender neutral* Greek word for "Spirit" (*pneuma*) and the *feminine* Greek word for "truth" (*alētheia*)—gender neutral and feminine.

However, the "he" mentioned before is the *gender neutral* Greek word *ekeinos*, which again is translated: he, *she*, it, etc. Every "he" after that is not actually a pronoun but is a verb (guiding, speaking, hearing, speaking, and showing) without reference to gender.

"Himself" is also *gender neutral*, the Greek word *heautou* meaning "himself, *herself*, itself, themselves."

So going back to the Greek, Holy Spirit is represented as either gender neutral or feminine in these scriptures, but we can see the assumption or bias of the translators, who referenced Holy Spirit *only* as *he/himself* seven times, six of those not even being in the original text.

After perusing many English translations, I could not find *one* that did not flow with this bias/presumption, even though the verbiage is all *gender neutral*, with a tipping toward the *feminine* with the word "truth" (*alētheia*).

I understand that "he" is generally used to cover all humanity, male and female. But I wonder how it would strike us if we instead used "she"—no less equal in the sight of God—to cover all of humanity for the next, oh say, six millennia or so, just to even things out. It makes me laugh just to think of it. After all, Eve was the mother of all living. It would certainly shake us out of our obliviousness.

Such masculine bias is the tip of the iceberg and is the water we swim in as Christ's little fishes, so we are blinded to the extent of it. This is sobering (and yet humorous) food for thought—perfect for engagement with Holy Spirit to lead us into all truth!

The Fruit of God and the Flesh

Another enlightening study is the fruit we bear as children of God, in our "lost-ness" and our "found-ness." Galatians 5 contrasts the works of the flesh with the fruit of the Spirit. How does this play out with the masculine and feminine?

Galatians 5:19–21 says:

> [19] *Now the **works** of the **flesh** are manifest, which are these; Adultery, fornication, uncleanness, lasciviousness,* [20] *Idolatry, witchcraft, hatred, variance, emulations, wrath, strife, seditions, heresies,* [21] *Envyings, murders, drunkenness, revellings, and such like: of the which I tell you before, as I have also told*

*you in time past, that they which do such things shall not inherit the **kingdom of God**.*

KJV (emphasis mine)

"Works" is the Greek word *ergon*, which is a *neuter* noun.

All the following are *feminine* nouns, and they comprise the majority:

"Flesh," "Adultery," "Fornication," "Uncleanness," "Lasciviousness/Lustfulness," "Idolatry," "Witchcraft," "Hatred," "Varience/Strife/Contention," "Strife," "Sedition/Dissension/Division," "Heresies," and "Drunkenness."[14]

What a line-up!

Interesting that the sexual sins and drunkenness are described in *feminine* terms. It is good to be kept on our toes!

The following are *masculine* or *masculine/neuter*:
"Emulations/Zeal/Rivalry/Jealousy," "Wrath," "Envyings," "Murders," and "Revelings/Rioting."[15]

---

14   "Flesh" is the Greek word *sarx*, a *feminine* noun.
"Adultery" is the Greek word *moicheia*, a *feminine* noun.
"Fornication" is the Greek word *porneia*, a *feminine* noun.
"Uncleanness" is the Greek word *akatharsia*, a *feminine* noun.
"Lasciviousness/Lustfulness" is the Greek word *aselgeia*, a *feminine* noun.
"Idolatry" is the Greek word *eidōlolatria*, a *feminine* noun.
"Witchcraft" is the Greek word *pharmakeia*, a *feminine* noun.
"Hatred" is the Greek word *echthra*, a *feminine* noun.
"Varience/Strife/Contention" is the Greek word *eris*, a *feminine* noun.
"Strife" is the Greek word *eritheia*, a *feminine* noun.
"Sedition/Dissension/Division" is the Greek word *dichostasia*, a *feminine* noun.
"Heresies" is the Greek word *hairesis*, a *feminine* noun.
"Drunkenness" is the Greek word *methē*, a *feminine* noun.
15   "Emulations/Zeal/Rivalry/Jealousy" is the Greek word *zēlos*, a *masculine/neuter* noun.
"Wrath" is the Greek word *thymos*, a *masculine* noun vs. *orge* in Romans 5.
"Envyings" is the Greek word *phthonos*, a *masculine* noun.
"Murders" is the Greek word *phonos*, a *masculine* noun.
"Revelings/Rioting" is the Greek word *kōmos*, a *masculine* noun.

This list is less than flattering for the female sex, that is, until we get to the happy part—the fruit of the Spirit. Once again, Holy Spirit comes to our collective human rescue—hallelujah! Galatians 5:22–23 says:

> *²² But the **fruit** of the **Spirit** is **love, joy, peace, longsuffering, gentleness, goodness, faith**, ²³ **Meekness, temperance**: against such there is no **law**.*   KJV (emphasis mine)

"Fruit" is the Greek word *karpos*, which is a *masculine* noun.
"Spirit" is the Greek word *pnuema*, which is a *neuter* noun.

The entirety of the fruit of the Spirit in expression is *feminine:*
    "Love," "Joy," "Peace," "Long-suffering/patience/endurance," "Gentleness/kindness," "Goodness," "Faith," "Meekness/Gentleness," and "Temperance/self-control."[16]

Interestingly, "Law" is the Greek word *nomos*, which is a *masculine* noun.

So, we see that "the works (neutral) of the flesh (feminine)" is expressed in *feminine* to *masculine* terms in a roughly 12:5 ratio. However, "the fruit (masculine) of the Spirit (neutral)" is entirely *feminine* in expression. It is striking that the theme of what is masculine or gender neutral being expressed in feminine terms is borne out repeatedly.

---

16   "Love" is the Greek word *agapē*, a *feminine* noun.
"Joy" is the Greek word *chara*, a *feminine* noun.
'Peace" is the Greek word *eirēnē*, a *feminine* noun.
"Long-suffering/patience/endurance" is the Greek word *makrothymia*, a *feminine* noun.
"Gentleness/kindness" is the Greek word *chrēstotēs*, a *feminine* noun.
"Goodness" is the Greek word *agathōsynē*, a *feminine* noun.
"Faith" is the Greek word *pistis*, a *feminine* noun.
"Meekness/Gentleness" is the Greek word *praotēs*, a *feminine* noun.
"Temperance/self-control" is the Greek word *egkrateia*, a *feminine* noun.

Pondering with Peter

A final study that is powerful and enlightening can be found in 2 Peter 1:2–4, which says:

> *² **Grace** and **peace** be multiplied to you in the **knowledge** of **God** and of **Jesus** our **Lord**, ³ as His divine **power** has given to us all things that pertain to **life** and **godliness**, through the **knowledge** of Him who called us by **glory** and **virtue**, ⁴ by which have been given to us exceedingly great and precious **promises**, that through these you may be **partakers** of the **divine nature**, having escaped the **corruption** that is in the world through **lust**.*
> NKJV (emphasis mine)

The balance of the masculine and feminine shakes out as follows. *Feminine* in Greek terms include:
"Grace," "Peace," "Knowledge," "Power," "Life," "Godliness," "Glory," "Virtue," "Corruption," and "Lust."[17]

Masculine terms are: "God," "Jesus" and "Lord," "partakers," and "world."[18]

"He" is the Greek word *autos*, a pronoun for: he, she, it, himself, herself, itself, and themselves. Thus, it is masculine (or feminine or neutral) at the preference of the translator.

---

17 "Grace" is the Greek word *charis*, a *feminine* noun.
"Peace" is the Greek word *eirēne*, a *feminine* noun.
"Knowledge" is the Greek word *epignōsis*, a *feminine* noun.
"Power" is the Greek word *dynamis*, a *feminine* noun.
"Life" is the Greek word *zōē*, a *feminine* noun.
"Godliness" is the Greek word *eusebeia*, a *feminine* noun.
"Glory" is the Greek word *doxa*, a *feminine* noun.
"Virtue" is the Greek word *aretē*, a *feminine* noun.
"Corruption" is the Greek word *phthora*, a *feminine* noun.
"Lust" is the Greek word *epithymia*, a *feminine* noun.
18 "God" is the Greek word *theos*, a *masculine* noun.
"Jesus" and "Lord" are the Greek word *kyrios* and are both *masculine* nouns.
"Partakers" is the Greek word *koinōnos*, a *masculine* noun.
"World" is the Greek word *kosmos*, a *masculine* noun.

"Promises" is the Greek word *epangelma*, which is a *gender neutral* noun.

"Divine nature" is actually an adjective without reference to gender.

It seems that the *feminine* nouns include ten lofty attributes alongside "corruption" and "lust." The *masculine* is mostly represented by "Father" and "Son."

Second Peter 1:5–7 is reminiscent of the fruit of the Spirit and reads:

> *⁵ But also for this very reason, giving all **diligence**, add to your **faith virtue**, to virtue **knowledge**, ⁶ to knowledge **self-control**, to self- control **perseverance**, to perseverance **godliness**, ⁷ to godliness **brotherly kindness**, and to brotherly kindness **love**.*
> NKJV (emphasis mine)

Feminine expression is unilateral:
"Diligence," "Faith," "Virtue," "Knowledge," "Temperance/self-control," "Patience," "Love," and "Godliness."[19]

"Godliness" is once again the Greek word *eusebeia*, which is a *feminine* noun. This is interesting since God, as Father and Son, is *masculine*, but to "be like" God is *feminine*.

"Brotherly kindness" is the Greek word *philadelphia*, which is a *feminine* noun. I find the term "brotherly" amusing, since it is *feminine*, and, thus, more aptly translated "sisterly kindness." But I vote for that type of love, whatever gender is credited with it!

Once again, and it could be ad nauseum if it weren't so delightful and gorgeous, the interplay between the masculine and feminine is seamlessly and beautifully intertwined.

---

19   "Diligence" is the Greek word *spoudē*, a *feminine* noun.
"Faith" is the Greek word *pistis*, a *feminine* noun.
"Virtue" is once again, the Greek word *aretē*, a *feminine* noun.
"Knowledge" is the Greek word *gnōsis*, a *feminine* noun.
"Temperance/self-control" is the Greek word *egkrateia*, a *feminine* noun.
"Patience" is the Greek word *hypomonē*, a *feminine* noun.
"Love" is the Greek word *agapē*, a *feminine* noun.

CHAPTER SIX
SUMMING UP

This study is not to confuse, blur, vilify, or negate masculinity and femininity—God forbid! We have enough gender confusion and pervasive bondage and fallout as a result. As with any area of confusion we have, particularly about identity, it is all the more imperative that we look to our ever-good, glorious, wise, *inclusive,* and lovely Creator to help us, and *not* to create Him/Her in our own image and according to our own hidden agendas (often hidden from ourselves). In our sinful ways of being (overt and covert) as men and women against one another and ourselves, we do need to be confronted—not because we are bad, but because in our truest selves, *we are so good,* just like our Father/Brother/Husband/Friend. We simply need to be and do better, worthy of who we truly are.

As horrific as we may act, we are not to be condemned. That is simply not justifiable (Rom. 8:1, Eph. 1:7, Col. 1:14, and Matt. 7:1–5). Nor are we to condemn one another. We need a *ton* of healing, and we can't heal if we are condemned. With that in mind, we are constantly being conformed into the image of Christ (Rom. 8:19 and 29–30), and thus, we *will* be convicted, sometimes seemingly brutally, of the righteousness (John 16:18 and Heb. 12:29) that looks like Love Him/Herself (1 John 4:8, 16; John 13:34). God empowers us to be and do better toward one another and ourselves (Phil. 2:13). Nothing less is worthy of God's beloved, gorgeous sons and daughters.

We are free to celebrate the beauty and mystery of *both* men and women as exquisitely completing the other and being intrinsically, equally honorable and invaluable—one not being over the other in any way! We are better together, seamlessly working and championing one another the way the Trinity does, both masculine and feminine.

So what are you saying, Catherine? Is God male or female? Let me repeat what God told me in His mandate to me:

> *I want you to teach on My dual feminine and masculine nature. I AM above the gender issue, and it is important that My kids*

grow in seeing Me rightly. I AM neither male nor female but engender both.

God is neither male nor female but transcends and engenders both. Both are prized and gorgeous! We can embrace who we are and champion one another—freed from gender battles. We, as God's sons and daughters, are on the same side—the side of Papa, Jesus, and Holy Spirit! And He/She is redeeming *all* things!

CHAPTER SEVEN

YOUR TURN: ENCOUNTERING GOD MASCULINE AND FEMININE

A theological study is wonderful and necessary for our spiritual and personal growth. However, it is what we refer to in the medical world as "necessary but not sufficient" if we want robust, fulfilling spiritual and personal lives. Unless study stirs the heart to encounter the One we are studying, we leave with knowledge in our minds, but we are unchanged in our intimacy with God, our identities, our ways of being, and our relationships with others. Knowledge informs, but encounter transforms. And after all, isn't transformation what we are after?

As regards the topic of this book, there areas in our own lives in which we need to be enlightened, healed, and upgraded as it relates to the masculine and feminine in our identities, our relationships, our marriages, our sexuality...pick a card, any card! Let's take some time to engage with God, Who is, as He/She stated, neither masculine nor feminine but engendering both. Papa/Jesus/Holy Spirit are wild about you and know what you need!

I have set forth a series of questions for you to engage with, seeking out your own heart and engaging with God's. As you talk to God, pause and rest. Practice attending to any thoughts, pictures in your mind, feelings, impressions, knowings, physical sensations, or other manifestations. Take your time! Write down what you are getting in a notepad or journal. Focus on the little that you think you *may* be "getting," and you will get more. Test it inwardly to see if it carries peace, a good feeling, authoritative weightiness, and any of the fruit of the Spirit (Gal. 5:22–23). This is how you practice discerning whether it is you, God, or "the demonic".

If you are not used to "hearing" from God, you can download my "How to Hear from God—An Experiential Journey" mini-book for free at: https://bit.ly/3cTNb49 (or you can also purchase it on Amazon). It is your birthright to hear/receive from God, and this practice (which takes *a lot* of practice—hint, hint) is non-negotiable for your spiritual growth and well-being. The sons/daughters of God are led by the Spirit of God living inside (Rom. 8:14). Relax and have fun with it. This is not about getting things perfectly. It's about connecting with the One Who loves you, will keep you safe, and will relentlessly lead you into all truth, wholeness, and freedom!

I'll pray first:

> Papa/Jesus/Holy Spirit,
>
> We thank You that You love us so passionately and completely.
> Thank You that You receive and affirm us as sons and daughters that You never leave, abandon, reject, or condemn.
> Thank You that You are our Healer, our Helper, our compassionate High Priest, our Mediator, our Redeemer, our Savior, and the One Who intercedes and empowers us continually.
>
> *You* are the One in Whom we live and move and have our being.
> You are the One Who knows us completely and adores us right where we are.
> You know our histories.
> You know our deepest, darkest tragedies, catastrophes, traumas, sinful ways of being, and sinful behaviors.
> You know our joys, achievements, creativity, and brilliance.
> You know our blindness, confusion, darkness, and delusions.
> You know our failures and hypocrisies, our beauty and our victories.
> You know it *all*, and you know *all* of us.
>
> *Thank You* for loving us so intricately and utterly.
> *Thank You* for your endless and oh-so-tender mercies that You renew day in and day out and that wholly triumph over judgment.
> *Thank You* for Your grace that abounds exceedingly over all sin.
> We come to You with the needs we know of and the needs

of which we are unaware.

We come to you with our strengths and understanding, our cluelessness and incompetence.

Help us, lovely Helper, to sense Your sweet and oh-so-safe presence.
Help us awaken to You—always with and in us, always loving us, and always there to guide and empower us.
Enlighten the eyes of our understanding, empowering our spiritual senses, minds, knowing, emotions, and bodies to connect with You.

We recognize that You engender both the masculine and feminine, and as such, there are things You want us to know about You, ourselves, and one another.
Thank You for helping us.

In Jesus' name, amen!

GOD ENCOUNTER BREAK

1. **As you were going through the book, what surprised you? What made you feel uncomfortable or unsure?**

   If you are sensing something but are not sure what it is, ask God. He/She knows exactly what is going on in your heart. Write down what you get (or what you think you are getting) in a notepad or journal. Remember, take the pressure off; you are practicing. This is not about your performance or perfection. It's about God's. He/She is a way better Teacher than you are a student. He/She is a way better Communicator than you are a receiver, and He/She is there to vastly help! Sometimes encounter with God feels more natural in a supernatural way and sometimes more dynamic. Anything you get, no matter how small, is wonderful and a treasure to guard; and you/He/She can build on it together! If something painful comes up, it is coming up to be healed. That means you are ready, *and* you are not alone! So rest, stay steady, and let things unfold. Write your thoughts here or in a journal/notepad.

   _____
   _____
   _____
   _____

Pray on your own or follow this prayer:

Papa/Jesus/Holy Spirit,

Thank You for helping me connect with my heart and Yours. Reveal what is going on in any place of discomfort or uncertainty. Wherever there is a fear or insecurity that has come up, reveal what is going on, and help me to track with what You are revealing. Thank You for reminding me that I am not alone—that You are here to help, empower, protect, and heal me.

In Jesus' name, amen!

Write anything you are or think you might be getting here or in your notepad/journal.

_____
_____
_____
_____
_____

Let me pray on your behalf:

> *Papa/Jesus/Holy Spirit,*
>
> *In this unsettled, insecure, or fearful place, what truth do You want Your son/daughter to know?*

Let God speak in words, thoughts, pictures, feelings, impressions, knowings, physical sensations, or other manifestations. Take your time! Write down what you are getting (or think you are getting) here or in a notepad or journal.

_____
_____
_____
_____
_____

Let me pray again on your behalf:

> *Papa/Jesus/Holy Spirit,*
>
> *In this unsettled, insecure, or fearful place, are there any <u>other</u> truths You want your son/daughter to know?*

Let God speak/minister to you again. Continue here until you feel all the fears/insecurities have been addressed and there is peace and write them here or in your journal/notepad.

_____
_____
_____
_____
_____

If you have more than you can do in one session, do what you can and set aside another time to come back to receive more. This is not a one-and-done process. You can always come back to these areas as much as you need if you need more ministry. God *always* desires to reassure, heal, and bring more and more truth that results in tangible freedom.

When you are at *complete* peace as you feel around inside regarding these areas, that is what healed feels like. Who knew, right? Be patient and kind with yourself and follow as God leads. You can and were designed to do this!

2. As you were going through the book, was there fear, hurt, anger, or resentment that came up?

Ask the Lord if there is anyone (singular or perhaps many, including institutions and genders) who you need to release in forgiveness. This could be yourself, God (yes, we get mad, disappointed, and disillusioned with Him/Her, even if He/She did not "sin"), an abuser or multiple abusers, your parents or other relatives, a spouse or romantic partner, a friend, a leader, a gender, the church...

Understand that forgiveness does not mean the harm was okay. It means that you are looking to *God* to heal, redeem, and restore. Those people/entities often could never make up for the harm they did, even if they wanted to. Only God can! And forgiveness releases that justice piece to Him. Forgiveness is for *your* freedom. And God empowers us supernaturally to forgive so that *we* can be free!

Otherwise, we will get stuck.

Spend some time resting here.

If God reveals someone/something to you, ask for His/Her grace (it may take a boatload, and that's okay) to release the anger, hurt, disillusionment, shame, damage, trauma, etc. to Him/Her.

Then say out loud, "As an act of my will, I choose to let _____ off the hook for _____, _____, _____, _____, _____, _____ . . . ."

List all of it, blow by blow as you need to. This gives you a voice in your place of pain, injury, anger, or rage. Let it be as raw, ugly, and irrational as it needs to be. The more you give yourself permission to connect with your heart and emotions, the more transformational this will be.

This is not the time to stay in your head, practice the "fruit of the Spirit," make excuses for anyone, or be understanding. It's time to come clean with what is *really* going on inside of you emotionally so that it can be healed. If it is ugly, that's okay! It is good because it is honest, and this is where you really live. You need to allow it to be brought up, to acknowledge it, and to allow all the emotions to come up for it to be healed. God will strengthen you, and you are not shocking God with anything—even if it is fury with Him/Her.

Often, it is helpful to list out all the ugly things and ways you were made to *feel*. For example, I forgive ____ for making me feel:
- Small
- Stupid
- Powerless/helpless
- Crazy
- Belittled
- Mocked
- Alone/abandoned/forsaken
- Discarded/used

- Taken advantage of
- Unacceptable/rejected
- Not enough
- Shameful/dirty
- Weak
- Evil
- Like a burden/in the way
- Like a loser
- Broken
- Hopeless
- Like a victim
- Incompetent
- Humiliated
- Weird/Different
- Ugly
- Incapacitated/traumatized
- Bullied
- Trapped
- Unsafe/in danger
- Terrorized/panicked
- Ashamed of my body
- Ashamed of my behavior/performance/failures
- Ashamed of my gender
- Ashamed of my sexuality
- For calling me ...

And/or anything else that comes up. Say,

> *I release all these things to You, Papa/ Jesus/ Holy Spirit, with all the trauma and weight they have brought me throughout my life. I hand You all the ways this has impacted how I see myself, my femininity/ masculinity, You, other men/ women, and the world.*

Rest and let Papa/ Jesus/ Holy Spirit help you release it to Him/ Her. He/She is the only One, Who can handle the toxicity. Papa/ Jesus/ Holy Spirit wants it, because that will unburden you and be a

huge part of your healing.
Now let me pray:

> *Papa/ Jesus/ Holy Spirit,*
>
> *Thank You for taking all that junk off Your beloved son/daughter. As You continue to minister, what truth do You want Your son/daughter to know?*

Let God speak in words, thoughts, pictures, feelings, impressions, knowings, physical sensations, or other manifestations. Take your time!

Write down what you are getting here or in your notepad or journal. Continue receiving truth and more truth as it comes.

This may be about masculinity/femininity, or it may not, but it is what you are supposed to receive now.

Allow God to reveal as many people/entities/institutions as necessary that need to be released, and then repeat the process. Make sure you ask God what truth He/She wants to reveal after you do so. Write down what you are getting here or in your notepad/journal.

_____
_____
_____
_____
_____
_____
_____
_____
_____
_____
_____
_____
_____
_____

3. **Ask Papa/ Jesus/ Holy Spirit to reveal any lies about masculinity/ femininity or any other related (or unrelated) areas that have been imprinted on your heart.**

Write them down what you are getting here or in your journal/notepad.

_____
_____
_____
_____
_____
_____
_____
_____

Ask Him/Her to minister truth in each area. Spend some time lingering here as you engage with the truth that you are getting and write it down in your journal/notepad.

_____
_____
_____
_____
_____
_____
_____
_____
_____

If the truth does not *feel* true, ask God if there are any other lies that are undermining your ability to rest in the truth that you are getting. Write them down, and then ask Him/Her what the truth is here. Let Him/Her minister that truth to you, and write it down below or in your journal/notepad.

_____
_____
_____
_____
_____
_____
_____
_____
_____
_____
_____
_____
_____

Repeat as much as needed. This is really a lifelong process, so embrace it and be patient. It is worth it because *you* are worth it!

Often in this process, you will find others you need to release in forgiveness. If so, do as you did above. The need to forgive can come up repetitively, even with people/ institutions/ genders/ etc. that you have already forgiven. You didn't do anything wrong for needing to forgive more (welcome to the authentic human race). There are just deeper levels of release for you to experience complete peace and freedom.

God's idea of freedom and wholeness is way greater than what most of us would settle for. Follow Him/Her. Papa/ Jesus/ Holy Spirit is relentless at bringing wholeness and freedom! Take as long as you need to, and feel free to come back again as much as you need.

4. Ask Papa/ Jesus/ Holy Spirit for forgiveness for the ways you have treated *Them/others.*

God has already *completely* forgiven you for *everything* you have done/ not done/ will do/ not do. But *receiving* His/Her forgiveness will help *you* feel clean and new. If you still feel defiled, ask God to cleanse your conscience with His/Her blood, and then stay there, allowing Him/Her to minister that cleansing (Heb. 9:14; 10:22). Write down what you are getting in the space below or in your journal/notepad.

5. Ask Papa/Jesus/Holy Spirit if there is anyone from whom you need to ask forgiveness for the ways you have treated *them*.

If there is someone else from whom you need to ask forgiveness, have God show you how and when to do this, and ask for His/Her empowerment to do so. People have a free will not to forgive you, but if they don't, that is on them. You are not responsible for their willingness, but your bravery here will create a space to draw them into eventual forgiveness that will free them.

If there are any amends you should make, ask about this as well, and ask for His/Her timing and empowerment to do so. This will require courage, but you are brave, and life is short. You will never regret following God, even in the super hard things. You will regret *not* doing so. You can ask God to help you to be willing (or to be willing to be willing). He/She is after healing our broken wills as well as our minds, emotions, personalities, and bodies. Write down what you are getting in the space below or in your journal/notepad.

_____
_____
_____
_____
_____
_____
_____
_____
_____
_____
_____
_____
_____
_____

6. Ask Papa/ Jesus/ Holy Spirit how They feel about you as Their son or daughter. This is *huge!*

Spend as much time as you can here, letting Him/Her *lavish* their love, approval, and joy over you (yes you)! Go back here frequently until this becomes easier and easier for you to seamlessly connect with! Write down what you are getting in the space below or in your journal/notepad.

You can come back anytime to these questions or similar ones that arise, using this as a launching pad for your own encounters. I cannot recommend enough the value of this type of brave, authentic, and intentional engagement. But a little dab will not do.

You will get better and better at this with practice and more practice. You will heal more and more and find your intimacy with God, yourself, and others skyrocketing even if it is a baby step at a time.

Now let me pray over you one final time:

Papa/Jesus/Holy Spirit,

Oh how You adore Your son/daughter just as You created and crafted them in Your image and likeness—so exquisitely unique, powerful, lovely, lovable, and full of promise and purpose. You are so proud of them for stretching and growing. I thank You for continuing to cause them to grow in the knowledge of You, of who You made them to be, and of the precious people and world around them. Thank You for the amazing fruit You are bearing in them, in their lives, and through them. And I thank You that they are Your delight and joy, and that they are growing in their ability to experience that.

In Jesus' name, amen!

Thank you so much for sharing this journey with me. It has been such a privilege, and I'd love to hear from you! Please feel free to contact me via the information following. Multiplied blessings on your journey!

Sending love,

Catherine

ABOUT THE AUTHOR

Catherine began her career as a board-certified Internal Medicine MD. She retired from medicine to raise her children and wholeheartedly pursue God's call on her life.

She has served in numerous capacities, including prayer, healing, wholeness and prophetic coaching, teaching, and equipping. She directed healing rooms, The Transformation Center, Encounter Ministries, and ran conferences. She has served on her church's senior leadership team and multiple boards, later directing Emerge Campus School of Transformation.

An ordained apostle and prophet, Catherine speaks forth vision, direction, confirmation, and practical strategic insight with piercing accuracy into individuals, leaders, and organizations around the globe. Her refreshing, unconventional way of introducing people to God's love has transformed the lives of thousands.

Catherine is the founder of Imprint, LLC, and Catherine Toon Ministries, which are dedicated to restoring wholeness, revealing identity, and releasing destiny through the unveiling of God's imprint of Love, uniquely expressed in every person.

In 2017, Catherine released her first book, *Marked by Love*. She followed up with a *Marked by Love* online course, workbook, and leaders' guide. Catherine has also authored *Rare and Beautiful Treasures* mini-book and *How to Hear God, An Experiential Journey*. And there are more books to come!

Her podcast, "Perspectives with Catherine Toon," is a popular breath of fresh air. She is a sought out speaker and coach. But her greatest joy is the simplicity of being adored by God, adoring Him back, while treasuring her husband and three children.

For more information or to subscribe to weekly prophetic words/blogs, visit Catherine's website at CatherineToon.com.

To request Catherine for speaking engagements, go online to CatherineToon.com/request.
To contact Catherine, email info@CatherineToon.com.

FIND CATHERINE:

Facebook: @CatherineToonMD
Instagram: @catherinetoon
YouTube: @Catherine Toon, MD
LinkedIn: @Catherine Toon
Pinterest: @catherinetoonmd
Twitter: @CatherineToonMD

Podcast: "Perspectives with Catherine Toon" on all major podcast platforms or CatherineToon.com/perspectives-with-catherine-toon-podcast

To contact Catherine: email info@CatherineToon.com

Blog: CatherineToon.com/blog

To find where Catherine is speaking: CatherineToon.com/events

To request Catherine for speaking engagements: CatherineToon.com/request

OTHER BOOKS BY CATHERINE:

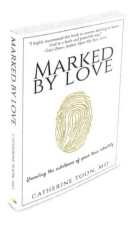

Marked by Love

Love is not only a powerful emotion, but it is a Person. This book provides an in-depth, ecstatic exploration of Love. You won't just read about love—Catherine will lead you to intimately encounter God as Love through the book with her "Love Encounter Break" exercises. In doing so, you will begin to unveil the way He has uniquely and exquisitely created and marked you. As you connect with who you truly are, you will be empowered to make your unique mark on a world that is starving for Love.

Are you tired of hearing about the love of God, only to find that it doesn't feel real? Love is our deepest emotional and spiritual need, and Love is a Person. God is Love. Without Him as the source of love, we shrivel up emotionally, spiritually, and physically. We limp through life. We have no idea who we really are or the ultimate reason we are on the planet. This workbook complements the acclaimed *Marked by Love* book and provides a Holy Spirit-guided adventure into experiencing the Person of Love.

Marked by Love Workbook

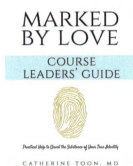

Marked by Love Leaders' Guide

This *Marked by Love* Leaders' Guide accompanies the *Marked by Love* Online Course, workbook, and critically-acclaimed book. It will equip and prepare you, step by step, to lead your group through Holy Spirit-guided adventures into experiencing the Person of Love. As you and your group are led into intimate encounters with Love, you will begin to unveil the exquisite ways that you have been created and marked by God. As you connect with who you truly are, you will be empowered to make your unique mark on a world that is starving for Love!

Do you want to hear God for yourself? Do you want to discover *your* unique way of hearing Him? If so, Catherine has put this book together just for *you!* Even if this is something you've been operating in for a long time, there is always a deeper experiential connection that the Lord wants with you. God wants to be known. He speaks and wants to be heard, and He has given you the inherent capacity to connect with Him. Catherine will help you with practical insights and keys to: uncover how God has uniquely wired you for connection, learn how to receive from Him in line with the way you are wired, become *confident* that you can hear from God, and more!

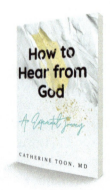

How to Hear from God

Rare and Beautful Treasures

This book is packed with practical insights and keys to: move from heartbreak to desires *fulfilled*, encounter God's true goodness toward you, become *confident* that you will experience transformation in your situations, *feel safe* with God, and experience all the treasures He has for your life. Find out how good God really is so you can receive *everything* you are looking for. See God *transform* the broken and ugly into something overwhelmingly powerful and strikingly beautiful. Buckle up your seat belts! It's time to encounter God. It is time to see the beauty of His treasures!

Interested in growing your relationsip with God more and want to use these tools as a way to do so?

All Books can be purchased on Amazon & Audible.

Or visit Catherine at catherinetoon.com/products

Don't forget the freebies!

CatherineToon.com/free-downloads

ONLINE MARKED BY LOVE COURSE

Are you tired of feeling stuck in the guilt trap—perhaps feeling confused and disconnected from God?

Imagine being secure and connected in your relationship with God in a way that creates peace and wholeness in every area of your life.

What if you could experience God *anytime*, *anyplace*, and *in any situation*? What if you knew how to hear His voice all the time? How would that impact your life, your relationships, and your future?

"Marked by Love" is an experiential course that will take you on a journey into the heart of Love. This course will touch the depths of your soul, and you will experience God in a way that you never thought possible.

For more online course information, go to mbl.CatherineToon.com/sales-landing